Zen Habits

Handbook for Life

Hundreds of Tips for Simplicity, Productivity and Happiness

by

Leo Babauta

Zen Habits – Handbook for Life

Copyright © 2009 by Leon H. Rountree III

ISBN 1-4414218-9-0

Table of Contents

Dedicated to my mom, Shannon, the best person I know

Introduction

When I first started out in my adult life, 17 years ago, it would have been nice if someone I respected had handed me a handbook, with all the essential topics covered in a how-to format.

It would have taught me to simplify my life, which I've learned to do in the last few years.

It would have talked about the essentials of happiness, and how to be productive and achieve my dreams.

Of course, life doesn't come with such a handbook, and not even the best of us could write a handbook that did an adequate job.

So this book is but a poor substitute for that. Because in truth, there can be no one set of instructions that will work for every single one of us. And in all honesty, it's so much better to learn by doing than to learn by reading.

But that doesn't stop me from trying. Zen Habits, my blog, has been my attempt to share things I've learned, the things that have worked for me as I have achieved successes these last few years:

- became a runner
- became vegetarian
- ran a marathon
- became organized and productive

- doubled my income
- completed a triathlon
- started a successful blog
- eliminated my debt
- lost 30 pounds
- sold a successful ebook
- became an early riser
- created a minimal home

When put all together, these sound like a lot of accomplishments in only a couple years. But it was just the simple application of a few principles, creating one habit at a time, learning to focus myself, and doing things that I love.

This book is simply a collection of some of my best articles from Zen Habits.

They are available for free on the blog, but I've collected them here at the request of readers. I hope they will be of some use to you ... choose the articles that apply best to your life, and give them a try.

- Leo Babauta, ZenHabits.net

Section 1:
Simplicity

Chapter 1:

Decluttering

One of the things that gives me most peace is have a clean, simple home. When I wake up in the morning and walk out into a living room that has been decluttered, that has a minimalist look, and there isn't junk lying around, there is a calm and joy that enters my heart.

When, on the other hand, I walk out into a living room cluttered with toys and books and extra things all over the place, it is chaos and my mind is frenetic.

I've been a simplifier and a declutterer for years now (probably 8-9 years) and I've gotten pretty good at it, but I've found that you have to keep coming back to revisit your clutter every once in awhile.

Here are my top decluttering tips:

- **Do it in small chunk**s. Set aside just 15 minutes to declutter just one shelf, and when that shelf or that 15 minutes is up, celebrate your victory. Then tackle another shelf for 15 minutes the next day. Conquering an entire closet or room can be overwhelming, and you might put it off forever. If that's the case, just do it in baby steps.

- **Set aside a couple hours to do it**. This may seem contradictory to the above tip ... and it is. It's simply a different strategy, and I say do whatever works for you. Sometimes, for me, it's good to set aside part of a morning, or an entire Saturday morning, to declutter a closet or room. I do it all at once, and when I'm done, it feels awesome.

- **Take everything out of a shelf or drawer at once.** Whichever of the two above strategies you choose, you should focus on one drawer or shelf at a time, and empty it completely. Then clean that shelf or drawer. Then, take the pile and sort it (see next tip), and put back just what you want to keep. Then tackle the next shelf or drawer.

- **Sort through your pile, one item at a time, and make quick decisions**. Have a trash bag and a give-away box handy. When you pull everything out of a shelf or drawer, sort through the pile one at a time. Pick up an item, and make a decision: trash, give away, or keep. Don't put it back in the pile. Do this with the entire pile, and soon, you'll be done. If you keep sorting through the pile, and re-sorting, it'll take forever. Put back only what you want to keep, and arrange it nicely.

- **Be merciless**. You may be a pack rat, but the truth is, you won't ever use most of the junk you've accumulated. If you haven't used it in the last year, get rid of it. It's as simple as that. If you've only used it once or twice in the last year, but know you won't use it in the next year, get rid of it. Toss it if it's unsalvageable, and give it away if someone else might be able to use it.

- **Papers? Be merciless, unless it's important.** Magazines, catalogues, junk mail, bills more than a year old, notes to yourself, notes from others, old work stuff ... toss it! The only exception is with tax-related stuff, which should be kept for seven years, and other important documents like warranties, birth and death and marriage certificates, insurance, wills, and other important documents like that. But you'll know those when you see 'em. Otherwise, toss!!!!

- **If you are on the fence with a lot of things, create a "maybe" box**. If you can't bear to toss something because you might need it later, put it in the box, then close the box, label it, and put it in storage (garage, attic, closet), out of sight. Most likely, you'll never open that box again. If that's the case, pull it out after six months or a year, and toss it or give it away.

- **Create a system to stop clutter from accumulating**. There's a reason you have tall stacks of papers all over the place, and big piles of toys and books and clothes. It's because you don't have a regular system to keep things in their place, and get rid of stuff you don't need. This is a topic for another day, but it's something to think about as you declutter. You'll never get to perfect, but if you think more intelligently about how your house got cluttered, perhaps you can find ways to stop it from happening again.

- **Celebrate when you're done!** This is actually a general rule in life: always celebrate your accomplishments, no matter how small. Even if you just decluttered one drawer, that's great. Treat yourself to something delicious. Open that drawer (or closet, or whatever), and admire its simplicity. Breathe deeply and know that you have done a good thing. Bask in your peacefulness.

Chapter 2:

Single-Tasking

You're working on two projects at once, while your boss has placed two new demands on your desk. You're on the phone while three new emails come in. You are trying to get out the door on time so you can pick up a few groceries on the way home for dinner. Your Blackberry is going off and so is your cell phone. Your co-worker stops by with a request for info and your Google Reader is filled with 100+ messages to read.

You are juggling tasks with a speed worthy of Ringling Bros. Congratulations, multitasker.

In this age of instant technology, we are bombarded with an overload of information and demands of our time. This is part of the reason GTD is so popular in the information world — it's a system designed for quick decisions and for keeping all the demands of your life in order. But even if we are using GTD, sometimes we are so overwhelmed with things to do that our system begins to fall apart.

This article is How NOT to Multi-task — a guide to working as simply as possible for your mental health.

First, a few quick reasons not to multi-task:

1. Multi-tasking is less efficient, due to the need to switch gears for each new task, and the switch back again.

2. Multi-tasking is more complicated, and thus more prone to stress and errors.

3. Multi-tasking can be crazy, and in this already chaotic world, we need to reign in the terror and find a little oasis of sanity and calm.

Here are some tips on how NOT to multi-task:

1. First set up to-do lists for different contexts (i.e. calls, computer, errands, home, waiting-for, etc.) depending on your situation.

2. Have a capture tool (such as a notebook) for instant notes on what needs to be done.

3. Have a physical and email inbox (as few inboxes as possible) so that all incoming stuff is gathered together in one place (one for paper stuff, one for digital).

4. Plan your day in blocks, with open blocks in between for urgent stuff that comes up. You might try one-hour blocks, or half-hour blocks, depending on what works for you. Or try this: 40 minute blocks, with 20 minutes in between them for miscellaneous tasks.

5. First thing in the morning, work on your Most Important Task. Don't do anything else until this is done. Give yourself a short break, and then start on your next Most Important Task. If you can get 2-3 of these done in the morning, the rest of the day is gravy.

6. When you are working on a task in a time block, turn off all other distractions. Shut off email, and the

Internet if possible. Shut off your cell phone. Try not to answer your phone if possible. Focus on that one task, and try to get it done without worrying about other stuff.

7. If you feel the urge to check your email or switch to another task, stop yourself. Breathe deeply. Re-focus yourself. Get back to the task at hand.

8. If other things come in while you're working, put them in the inbox, or take a note of them in your capture system. Get back to the task at hand.

9. Every now and then, when you've completed the task at hand, process your notes and inbox, adding the tasks to your to-do lists and re-figuring your schedule if necessary. Process your email and other inboxes at regular and pre-determined intervals.

10. There are times when an interruption is so urgent that you cannot put it off until you're done with the task at hand. In that case, try to make a note of where you are (writing down notes if you have time) with the task at hand, and put all the documents or notes for that task together and aside (perhaps in an "action" folder or project folder). Then, when you come back to that task, you can pull out your folder and look at your notes to see where you left off.

11. Take deep breaths, stretch, and take breaks now and then. Enjoy life. Go outside, and appreciate nature. Keep yourself sane.

Chapter 3:
Edit Your Commitments

I'm a former newspaper editor, and one of the things I learned was to edit brutally (no sarcastic comments about why I don't do that with my blog posts). Cut out everything that's not necessary, and you've got a more meaningful story.

I highly recommend editing your life.

Today's edit: All the commitments in your life.

Take an inventory of the commitments in your life. Here are some common ones:

- **Work** - we have multiple commitments at our jobs. List them all.

- **Side work** - some of us free-lance, or do odd jobs to take in money. More commitments.

- **Family** - we may play a role as husband, wife, father, mother, son, daughter. These roles come with many commitments.

- **Kids** - my kids have soccer, choir, Academic Challenge Bowl, National Junior Honor Society, basketball, spelling bee, and more. Each of their commitments is mine too.

- **Civic** - we may volunteer for different organizations, or be a board member or officer on a non-profit organization.

- **Religious** - many of us are very involved with our churches, or are part of a church organization. Or perhaps we are committed to going to service once a week.

- **Hobbies** - perhaps you are a runner or a cyclist, or you build models, or are part of a secret underground comic book organization. These come with - surprise! - commitments.

- **Home** - aside from regular family stuff, there's the stuff you have to do at home.

- **Online** - we may be a regular on a forum or mailing list or Google group. These are online communities that come with commitments too.

You might have other categories. List everything.

Now take a close look at each thing on the list, and consider: How does this give my life value? How important is it to me? Is it in line with my life priorities and values? How would it affect my life if I dropped out? Does this further my life goals?

These are tough questions, but I suggest seeing if you can eliminate just one thing — the thing that gives you the least return for your invested time and effort. The thing that's least in line with your life values and priorities and goals. Cut it out, at least for a couple weeks, and see if you can get along without it. Revisit this list at that time and see if you can cut something else out. Edit mercilessly, keeping only those that really mean something to you.

Each time you cut a commitment, it may give you a feeling of guilt, because others want you to keep that commitment. But it's also a huge relief, not having to do that commitment each day or week or month. It frees up a lot of your time, and while others may be disappointed, you have to keep what's important to you in mind, not everyone else. If we committed to what everyone else wanted all the time, we would never have any time left for ourselves.

Take the time to edit your commitments, and your life will be greatly simplified. You will thank yourself for it.

Chapter 4:
Eliminate All But the Essentials

If you're like me, you have a long list of tasks to do, perhaps broken down by different contexts (work, home, errands, calls, etc.). Your list of tasks is so long that it's overwhelming. You can never completely wipe out your list because it's growing every day.

Simplify your list down to the barest of essentials, and you can eliminate the need for complex planning systems.

Let's first imagine the ideal scenario. Recently I've begun simplifying my time management system from GTD down to basically nothing. I still have long lists of things to do, but I don't look at them much anymore. Instead, I've begun the process of elimination, and focusing on what's really important.

Now my to-do list is basically one list of three essential things I want to do today. I also have a list of a few smaller tasks that I want to knock out, all at once, usually in about 30 minutes or so, leaving the rest of my day free for the more important tasks. I still use my calendar, just as a way of reminding me of appointments, but it's not really a time management tool. I don't need time management tools anymore — I've simplified my list down to three tasks, every day.

How can you get to this point?

Here are the key steps:

- **Eliminate, eliminate**. Take a few minutes to review your task and project lists, and see how much you can simplify them. Make it a challenge. See if you can cut it in half! If you've got 50 items, cut it down to 25. Then try to cut it even further a few days later. How do you eliminate tasks? Sometimes a task gets old and isn't necessary anymore. Cross those out. Sometimes a task can be delegated. Do that, and cross it out. Read on for more tips.

- **Know what's essential**. How do you know what's essential? By knowing what your main goal is, and other goals if necessary. You really should focus on one goal at a time, but if you want to do 2 or 3, that's OK too. Just don't do 10 goals or anything. Those goals should be your essential projects. Any smaller tasks are essential if they help you accomplish those goals, and not essential if they're not related.

- **Simplify your commitments**. How many projects are you committed to? How many extracurricular stuff do you do? You can't do it all. You need to learn to say no, and value your time. And if you've already said yes, it's still possible to say no. Just be honest with people and tell them that you have a high number of urgent projects to complete and cannot commit to this any longer. Slowly, you can eliminate your commitments to a very small number — only have those commitments in your life that really give you joy and value.

- **Simplify your information stream**. I've recently gone through the process of eliminating most of my RSS feeds. I also have cut back on the number of emails I respond to. And for more than a year now, I haven't read a single newspaper, watched television (except DVDs), or read a single magazine. The news no longer gives me any value. Simplify the inputs into your life, and you can simplify the outputs.

- **Review weekly**. Your to-do list tends to build up over the course of a week. Take a few minutes each week to eliminate, and eliminate some more. You don't need a huge to-do list to be productive — just do the stuff that matters.

- **Big Rocks**. During your weekly review, figure out the most important tasks that you'd like to accomplish over the next week. Those are your Big Rocks. Now place them on your schedule, first thing in the day, on different days of the upcoming week. Make those the most important tasks each day, and do them first — don't let them be pushed back to the end of the day.

- **Biggest value**. Consider the case of two newspaper writers. One is super busy and writes a dozen articles a week. They're all decent articles, but they're pretty routine in nature. The second writer writes one article this week, but it gets the front page headline, it's talked about all around town and blogged about on the Internet, it gets him a journalism award and he becomes a big name in journalism. From this article, he lands a bigger job and a book deal. That example is a bit extreme, but it illustrates the point that some tasks really pay off in the long term, and others just keep you busy and in the long run, don't matter at all. The first writer could have stayed home all week and slept, and it wouldn't have changed his world much (except he wouldn't get paid for that week). Focus on those big tasks, that will make a name for you, that will generate long-term income, that will give you lasting satisfaction and happiness. Those are your Big Rocks. Eliminate the rest.

- **Three MITs**. Here's your planning system each day: write down your three Most Important Tasks on a sheet of paper (I write mine in a Moleskine pocket notebook). That's it. Check off those tasks when you finish them. Devote your entire day, if possible, to those three tasks, or at the very least devote the first half of your day to them. Your MITs are basically the Big Rocks you planned for this week, and any other MIT that you need to do for today.

- **Batch small tasks**. During the course of the day, other stuff will come up that you really need to take care of or they could create problems for you later. Write those down on another small list of small tasks (mine is at the bottom of my pocket notebook page). You don't need to do them right now, most likely. Just write them down for later. Set a time (probably 30 minutes or so) to batch process these tasks sometime later in the day (perhaps 4 p.m.). Do your MITs first, and then do all the small tasks at the same time. These might be calls, emails, writing a short letter, doing paperwork, etc. Try to do them quickly and knock them off your list. You might have a few tasks left at the end of the day. Better to leave the small tasks until tomorrow than the big ones. Batch process email, too — if you do it throughout the day, it's just a bunch of interruptions. Just do it once or twice a day.

Chapter 5:
Don't Do Everything on Your To-do List

A reader of Zen Habits, Jeremy Martin, wrote in with this question:

"My problem is that if I have a list of things to do, no matter if they are high priority or personal projects for myself, I feel guilty if I am not working to shrink that list. This can lead to periods of burnout for me, where I barely get anything done. I never know when it is okay to relax, or when it is okay to take a break and play that video game, read a book, or some other leisure activity. "

"Do you have any tips that might help me out?"

This problem is one that many of us deal with, and there's no easy answer. Here are my suggestions:

1. Set 1-3 Most Important Things (MITs) for the day. The top 1, 2, or 3 things that you really want to get done that day. This is an addition to the GTD system, not a part of it, but I find it helps me to focus on what's important. GTD assumes that you will know what needs to be done, which is true, but it's helpful to determine that at the beginning of each day, and make sure you get those things done.

2. Get your MITs done early in the day. Then everything else you do is extra. And if you feel like taking a break and playing, after you do the MITs, you can do this without worrying that you're not getting important stuff done.

3. You'll never get to the bottom of your list. This is something I had to learn the hard way. I would try to clear one of my

context lists (like @calls), but as soon as I crossed 2-3 off my list, another 2-3 would pop up. Now, I try to just get my list down to a reasonable number if possible.

4. GTD isn't about doing everything on your list. It's about knowing what needs to be done, so that when you're doing something else, you know that everything else that needs to be done, at some point, is accounted for in your system, and you don't need to worry about all that other stuff at this point. In other words, get all that stuff out of your head, and into your trusted system, so you don't have to worry about it while you focus on the task before you.

5. It's also good to schedule time blocks. I will set a block for email and calls, another for writing, another for interviews (a big part of my job), etc ... this way, I just try to get as much done in that block as possible, and then not worry about the rest until tomorrow's block. This is also not a part of GTD, but a useful addition, as GTD doesn't really advocate scheduling. But without a little bit of scheduling, as you've found, it can get a bit stressful, because you never know what needs to be done.

6. In the end, you can try these methods out, but you'll have to find what works for you. Some of these tips might work, some might not be for you. It's our systems that have to adapt to us, not the other way around!

Chapter 6:
The Art of Doing Nothing

Sure, we all know how to do nothing. We all know how to lay around and waste time. But many of us are too busy to do it much, and when we do it, our minds are often on other things. We cannot relax and enjoy the nothingness.

Doing nothing can be a waste of time, or it can be an art form. Here's how to become a master, and in the process, improve your life, melt away the stress and make yourself more productive when you actually do work.

Start small

Doing nothing, in the true sense of the word, can be overwhelming if you attempt to do too much nothing at once. Do small nothings at first. Focus on 5-10 minutes at a time, and start your practice sessions in a safe place — at home, not at work or in a busy public place. You may also not be ready to do nothing in the middle of nature, so do it in your bedroom or living room. Find a time and place where there are not many distractions, not much noise, not a lot of people to bother you.

Shut off all distractions

TV, computer, cell phones, regular phones, Blackberries, and the like. Doing nothing is hard when our communications gadgets are calling at us to do something.

Now, close your eyes, and do nothing. Yes, the smart-asses out there will say you're doing something — you're sitting there or laying there, closing your eyes. But we mean doing nothing in the sense that if someone were to call us up and ask what we're doing, we say "Oh, nothing." Don't let them call you up, though. They are trying to distract you.

After 5-10 minutes of doing, nothing, you can quit, and go do something. But try to do this every day, or as much as possible, because it is not possible to become a master without practice.

Breathing

The first place to start in the quest for mastery over this art is in your breathing. If this sounds suspiciously like meditation, well, cast those suspicions out of your mind. We are not here to do suspicion — we are doing nothing.

Start first by breathing slowly in, and then slowly out. Now closely monitor your breath as it enters your body, through your nose, and goes down into your lungs, and fills your lungs. Now feel it as it goes out of your body, through your mouth, and feel the satisfying emptying of your lungs.

Do this for 5-10 minutes, if you can. Practice this as you can. When you start thinking about other things, such as how great that darn Zen Habits blog is, well, stop that! Don't beat yourself up about it, but bring your thoughts back to your breathing every time.

Relaxing

An important part of doing nothing is being able to completely relax. If we are tense, then the doing of the nothing is really for naught. Relaxing starts by finding a comfortable place to do your nothing — a soft chair, a plush couch, a well-made, clean bed. Once you've found this spot, lie in it, and wiggle around to make it fit your body better. Think of how a cat lies down, and makes itself comfortable. Cats are very, very good at doing nothing. You may never approach their level of mastery, but they make for great inspiration.

Next, try the breathing technique. If you are not completely relaxed by now (and a short nap would be a great indication of relaxation), then try self massage. Yes, massage is much better when administered by other hands, but self massage is great too. Start with your shoulders and neck. Work your way up to your head and even your face. Also do your back, and legs and arms. Avoid any areas that might lead to doing something (although that can be relaxing too).

Yet another great way of relaxing is an exercise where you tense each muscle in your body, one body part at a time, and then let the tensed muscle relax. Start with your feet, then your legs, and work your way up to your eyebrows. If you can do the top of your head, you may be too advanced for this article.

Once you are relaxed, see if you can relax even more. Try not to relax so much that you lose control of your bodily fluids.

Bathing - an advanced stage

Those who are in the beginning stages of the Art of Doing Nothing should not attempt this stage. But once you've become proficient at the above steps, the stage of the Bath can be pretty great.

The bath must be nice and hot. Not lukewarm, but hot. Bubbles are also required, even if you are a man who is too manly for this. Just don't tell any of your guy friends. Other bath accessories, such as a loofah sponge, or bath gels, or potpourri, are very optional.

Again, you must have all distractions shut off. Bathing is also best done if you are alone in the house, but if not, everyone else in the house must know that you CANNOT be disturbed, even if the house is burning down. If they break this sacred rule, you must turn upon them with the Wrath of Hell(tm).

Step into your bath, one foot at a time, very slowly. If your bath is properly hot, it is best if you get into it an inch at a time. For more sensitive body parts, such as the crotch area, it is best to squeeze your eyes shut tight and slowly lower yourself into the steaming water despite all instincts to flee. Once you are fully immersed (and you should go completely under, head included, at first), close your eyes, and feel the heat penetrating your body.

You may begin to sweat. This is a good thing. Allow the sweat to flow. You may need a glass of water as the sweat could dehydrate you. A good book is another great way to enjoy your bath. Allow your muscles to be penetrated by the heat, to be relaxed completely, and feel all your worries and stresses and aches and inner turmoil flow out of your body into the water.

A hot bath is even more awesome if followed by a bracing cold shower. Either way, get out of the bath once the water is no longer warm and your skin is very raisin-like.

Tasting and feeling

Doing nothing is also great when accompanied by very good beverages or food. Good tea or coffee, wine, hot cocoa, and other sensual beverages go very well with the Art. It's best to take these beverages by themselves, with no food, and without a book or other distractions. Focus on the liquid as you sip it slowly, savoring every bit of the flavor and texture and temperature in your mouth before swallowing, and feeling the swallow completely. Close your eyes as you do this. Truly enjoy this drink.

Foods are also great: berries, rich desserts, freshly made bread, the best ... soup ... ever, or whatever it is that you love. Be sure you eat it slowly, savoring every bite. Chew slowly, and close your eyes as you enjoy the food. Feel the texture in your mouth. It is bliss!

Doing nothing in nature

Once you've passed the above stages, it is time to practice this gentle art out in nature. Find a peaceful place — in your front yard if that's peaceful, a park, the woods, at the beach, a river, a lake — places with water are excellent. Places out of reach of the sounds of traffic and city life are best.

Out here in nature, you can practice the art for 20 minutes, an hour, or even longer. There are fewer distractions, and you can really shut yourself off from the stresses of life. Don't just let your mind wander everywhere — focus on the natural surroundings around you. Look closely at the plants, at the water, at the wildlife. Truly appreciate the majesty of nature, the miracle of life.

Incorporating the Art in daily life

This is the final stage of mastering this Art. Don't attempt it until you've practiced and become competent at the above stages.

Start by doing nothing while you are waiting in line, at the doctor's office, on a bus, or for a plane. Wait, without reading a newspaper or magazine, without talking on the phone, without checking your email, without writing out your to-do list, without doing any work, without worrying about what you need to do later. Wait, and do nothing. Concentrate on your breathing, or try one of the relaxation techniques above. Concentrate on those around you — watch them, try to 19understand them, listen to their conversations.

Next, try doing nothing when you drive. Yes, you must drive, but try to do nothing else. Don't listen to music or news or an audiotape. Don't multi-task. Don't talk on your cell phone, don't eat, and don't do your makeup. Just drive. Concentrate on your driving, look at the things you are passing, and feel your breathing. Relax yourself, and don't worry about the other drivers (but don't crash into them!). Drive slowly, going easy on the gas and brake pedals. This technique has a great side-effect: better gas mileage.

Last, try doing nothing in the middle of chaos, in your workplace or other stressful environment. Just shut everything out, close your eyes, and think about your breathing. Try a relaxation technique. Do this for 5-10 minutes at a time, building up to 20-30 minutes. If you can do this, in the middle of a stressful day at work or with the kids, you will allow yourself to focus more fully on the task at hand. You will be relaxed and ready to concentrate, to bring yourself into a state of flow. (Warning: Doing nothing could get you in trouble with your boss, so be careful! But if it makes you more productive, you boss might not mind.)

Finally, the Art of Doing Nothing cannot be mastered overnight. It will take hours and hours of practice, of hard work (doing nothing isn't easy!). But you will enjoy every minute of it! Try it today.

Chapter 7:
Declutter Your Mind

"I fear I am not in my perfect mind." - King Lear

The world of stresses and worries and errands and projects and noise that we must all endure inflicts upon us a mind full of clutter and chaos.

A mind that sometimes cannot find the calm that we so desperately seek.

I've had a number of readers write to me, thanking me for my articles on decluttering ... but asking me, sometimes with a hint of despair, to write about decluttering your mind, not just your home or your desk.

It's a valid request — if anything needs decluttering, it's our minds, I think — but it's also a daunting task. How do you declutter a mind? It's not as if thoughts are just laying around, waiting for you to pick through them, finding the ones that should be kept and those that are ripe for the donation box. The mind isn't like an inbox, that can be sorted through and acted upon.

The brain is a complex and confusing organ, the core of us as human beings (if you feel, as I often do, that the soul is in the mind and not in the heart). The mind is often covered in the scar tissue of old hurts and traumas, and layered in so many levels of consciousness not even the best of psychoanalysts has ever sorted through it.

So how do we begin decluttering? It's actually not difficult, if you give it a little thought: simplifying shouldn't be made complex.

You can declutter your mind with simple actions, things we've discussed here before, but things that are almost guaranteed to have a positive effect. Little things that can make a big difference, especially when used in combination. Choose a few to try out, and see if they work for you.

1. **Breathe**. So simple, and yet so effective. Take a few deep breaths, and then for a few minutes, just focus on your breathing. Concentrate on your breathing as it comes into your body, and then as it goes out. It has a calming effect, especially if you continue to return your focus to your breath when your mind strays. It also allows other thoughts to just float away. (Note: some people might call this meditation, but that word scares some people off, so we're just going to call it breathing.)

2. **Write it down**. If you have a bunch of things on your mind, it helps to get them on paper and off your mind. This is one of the essential habits in Zen To Done (and GTD, of course) ... writing down your tasks and ideas. This keeps your head from being filled with everything you need to do and remember.

3. **Identify the essential**. This one is practically a mantra here at Zen Habits. (Can you imagine it? All of us here at Zen Habits, sitting on a mat in lotus position, chanting slowly: "Identify the essential ... identify ... the essen ... tial ...") But that's because it's crucial to everything I write about: if you want to simplify or

declutter, the first step is identifying what is most important. In this case, identify what is most important in your life, and what's most important for you to focus on right now. Make a short list for each of these things.

4. **Eliminate**. Now that you've identified the essential, you can identify what's not essential. What things in your life are not truly necessary or important to you? What are you thinking about right now that's not on your short list? By eliminating as many of these things as possible, you can get a bunch of junk off your mind.

5. **Journal**. Similar to "write it down" above, but with a little more depth. Journaling (whether it's in a paper journal or online doesn't matter) helps you explore different areas of your life that you don't think about much. And this exploration might allow you to find some things on your mind that you didn't realize were there, some things that can be eliminated or pursued. And just getting these thoughts into some kind of a journal is a way of getting them out of your mind as well.

6. **Rethink your sleep**. Sometimes we aren't getting enough sleep, or our sleeping patterns aren't ideal. I'm not saying that you should change your sleeping patterns, but sometimes it can do wonders. And if you don't give it some thought, you won't realize how much your sleep (or lack thereof) is affecting you.

7. **Take a walk**. Getting outside and doing some kind of physical activity is a great way to get stuff off your mind. I like to run or do yard work, but whatever you do doesn't matter. Spending some physical energy

31

clears the mind.

8. **Watch less TV**. For me, television doesn't relax me, although it might seem that vegging in front of the TV is good for relaxation. TV fills your head with noise, without the redeeming qualities of music or reading or good conversation. Watch less TV, and you'll notice your mind begin to quieten.

9. **Get in touch with nature**. Similar to "take a walk" above, but without the bustle of activity. I like to go somewhere with water ... the ocean, a river, a lake, even just a man-made fountain if nothing else is available. Or watching rain does the trick for me too. Somehow this can be calming and focusing at the same time.

10. **Do less**. Take your to-do list and cross off half the things on it. Just pick a few things to get done today, and focus on those. Let the rest go away. If you do less, you'll have less on your mind.

11. **Go slower**. Seems kinda weird, I know, but walking and talking and working and driving slower can make a very big difference. It's kind of like you're saying, "I'm not willing to rush through life, no matter what artificial time demands others are putting on me. I want to take it at my pace." And as a result, your mind is less harried as well.

12. **Let go**. Worrying about something? Angry about somebody? Frustrated? Harboring a grudge? While these are all natural emotions and thoughts, none of them are really necessary. See if you can let go of them. More difficult than it sounds, I know, but it's

worth the effort.

13. **Declutter your surroundings**. I've mentioned this before, but decluttering my desk or my home have a way of calming me. Having a lot of stuff around you is just visual clutter — it occupies part of your mind, even if you don't realize it.

14. **Single-task**. Multi-tasking, for the most part, is a good way to fill your mind with a lot of activity without a lot of productivity or happiness as a result. Instead, try to single-task — just focus on one task at a time. Clear away everything else, until you're done with that task. Then focus on the next task, and so on.

15. **Get a load off**. Sometimes it can make a huge difference to unload our troubles on another human being. If you have a significant other or a best friend or a close family member or coworker ... unload your thoughts on them. And listen to them, to return the favor. Sure, it's just talk ... but it can make a huge difference to your mental sanity.

Chapter 8:
72 Simplicity Tips

"Simplicity is the peak of civilization." Jessie Sampter

A simple life has a different meaning and a different value for every person. For me, it means eliminating all but the essential, eschewing chaos for peace, and spending your time doing what's important to you.

It means getting rid of many of the things you do so you can spend time with people you love and do the things you love. It means getting rid of the clutter so you are left with only that which gives you value.

However, getting to simplicity isn't always a simple process. It's a journey, not a destination, and it can often be a journey of two steps forward, and one backward.

If you're interested in simplifying your life, this is a great starter's guide (if you're not interested, move on).

The Short List

For the cynics who say that the list below is too long, there are really only two steps to simplifying:

1. **Identify what's most important to you.**
2. **Eliminate everything else.**

Of course, that's not terribly useful unless you can see how to apply that to different areas of your life, so I present to you the Long List.

The Long List

There can be no step-by-step guide to simplifying your life, but I've compiled an incomplete list
of ideas that should help anyone trying to find the simple life. Not every tip will work for you — choose the ones that appeal and apply to your life.

One important note: this list will be criticized for being too complicated, especially as it provides a bunch of links. Don't stress out about all of that. Just choose one at a time, and focus on that. When you're done with that, focus on the next thing.

1. **Make a list of your top 4-5 important things**.
    What's most important to you? What do you value most? What 4-5 things do you most want to do in your life? Simplifying starts with these priorities, as you are trying to make room in your life so you have more time for these things.

2. **Evaluate your commitments**. Look at everything you've got going on in your life. Everything, from work to home to civic to kids' activities to hobbies to side businesses to other projects. Think about which of these really gives you value, which ones you love doing. Which of these are in line with the 4-5 most important things you listed above? Drop those that aren't in line with those things.

3. **Evaluate your time**. How do you spend your day? What things do you do, from the time you wake up to the time you go to sleep? Make a list, and evaluate whether they're in line with your priorities. If not, eliminate the things that aren't, and focus on what's

important. Redesign your day.

4. **Simplify work tasks**. Our work day is made up of an endless list of work tasks. If you simply try to knock off all the tasks on your to-do list, you'll never get everything done, and worse yet, you'll never get the important stuff done. Focus on the essential tasks and eliminate the rest.

5. **Simplify home tasks**. In that vein, think about all the stuff you do at home. Sometimes our home task list is just as long as our work list. And we'll never get that done either. So focus on the most important, and try to find ways to eliminate the other tasks (automate, eliminate, delegate, or hire help).

6. **Learn to say no**. This is actually one of the key habits for those trying to simplify their lives. If you can't say no, you will take on too much.

7. **Limit your communications**. Our lives these days are filled with a vast flow of communications: email, IM, cell phones, paper mail, Skype, Twitter, forums, and more. It can take up your whole day if you let it. Instead, put a limit on your communications: only do email at certain times of the day, for a certain number of minutes (I recommend twice a day, but do what works for you). Only do IM once a day, for a limited amount of time. Limit phone calls to certain times too. Same with any other communications. Set a schedule and stick to it.

8. **Limit your media consumption**. This tip won't be for everyone, so if media consumption is important to you, please skip it (as with any of the other tips). However,

I believe that the media in our lives — TV, radio, Internet, magazines, etc. — can come to dominate our lives. Don't let it. Simplify your life and your information consumption by limiting it. Try a media fast.

9. **Purge your stuff**. If you can devote a weekend to purging the stuff you don't want, it feels seriously terrific. Get boxes and trash bags for the stuff you want to donate or toss.

10. **Get rid of the big items**. There's tons of little clutter in our lives, but if you start with the big items, you'll simplify your life quickly and in a big way.

11. **Edit your rooms**. One room at a time, go around the room and eliminate the unnecessary. Act as a newspaper editor, trying to leave only the minimum, and deleting everything else.

12. **Edit closets and drawers**. Once you've gone through the main parts of your rooms, tackle the closets and drawers, one drawer or shelf at a time.

13. **Simplify your wardrobe**. Is your closet bursting full? Are your drawers so stuffed they can't close (I'm talking about dresser drawers here, not underwear). Simplify your wardrobe by getting rid of anything you don't actually wear. Try creating a minimal wardrobe by focusing on simple styles and a few solid colors that all match each other.

14. **Simplify your computing life**. If you have trouble with too many files and too much disorganization, consider online computing. It can simplify things

greatly.

15. **Declutter your digital packrattery**. If you are a digital packrat, and cannot seem to control your digital clutter, there is still hope for you. Read this guide to curing yourself of this clutter.

16. **Create a simplicity statement**. What do you want your simple life to look like? Write it out.

17. **Limit your buying habits**. If you are a slave to materialism and consumerism, there are ways to escape it. I was there, and although I haven't escaped these things entirely, I feel much freer of it all. If you can escape materialism, you can get into the habit of buying less. And that will mean less stuff, less spending, less freneticism.

18. **Free up time**. Find ways to free up time for the important stuff. That means eliminating the stuff you don't like, cutting back on time wasters, and making room for what you want to do.

19. **Do what you love**. Once you've freed up some time, be sure to spend that extra time doing things you love. Go back to your list of 4-5 important things. Do those, and nothing else.

20. **Spend time with people you love**. Again, the list of 4-5 important things probably contains some of the people you love (if not, you may want to re-evaluate). Whether those people are a spouse, a partner, children, parents, other family, best friends, or whoever, find time to do things with them, talk to them, be intimate with them (not necessarily in sexual ways).

21. **Spend time alone**. See this list of ways to free up time for yourself — to spend in solitude. Alone time is good for you, although some people aren't comfortable with it. It could take practice getting used to the quiet, and making room for your inner voice. It sounds new-agey, I know, but it's extremely calming. And this quiet is necessary for finding out what's important to you.

22. **Eat slowly**. If you cram your food down your throat, you are not only missing out on the great taste of the food, you are not eating healthy. Slow down to lose weight, improve digestion, and enjoy life more.

23. **Drive slowly**. Most people rush through traffic, honking and getting angry and frustrated and stressed out. And endangering themselves and others in the meantime. Driving slower is not only safer, but it is better on your fuel bill, and can be incredibly peaceful. Give it a try.

24. **Be present**. These two words can make a huge difference in simplifying your life. Living here and now, in the moment, keeps you aware of life, of what is going on around you and within you. It does wonders for your sanity.

25. **Streamline your life**. Many times we live with unplanned, complex systems in our lives because we haven't given them much thought. Instead, focus on one system at a time (your laundry system, your errands system, your paperwork system, your email system, etc.) and try to make it simplified, efficient, and written. Then stick to it.

26. **Create a simple mail & paperwork system**. If you don't have a system, this stuff will pile up. But a simple system will keep everything in order.

27. **Create a simple system for house work**. Another example of a simple system is clean-as-you-go with a burst.

28. **Clear your desk**. If you have a cluttered desk, it can be distracting and disorganized and stressful. A clear desk, however, is only a couple of simple habits away.

29. **Establish routines**. The key to keeping your life simple is to create simple routines.

30. **Keep your email inbox empty**. Is your email inbox overflowing with new and read messages? Do the messages just keep piling up? If so, you're normal — but you could be more efficient and your email life could be simplified with a few simple steps.

31. **Learn to live frugally**. Living frugally means buying less, wanting less, and leaving less of a footprint on the earth. It's directly related to simplicity. Here are 50 tips on how to live frugally.

32. **Make your house minimalist**. A minimalist house has what is necessary, and not much else. It's also extremely peaceful (not to mention easy to clean).

33. **Find other ways to be minimalist**. There are tons. You can find ways to be minimalist in every area of your life.

34. **Consider a smaller home**. If you rid your home of stuff, you might find you don't need so much space. I'm not saying you should live on a boat (although I know some people who happily do so), but if you can be comfortable in a smaller home, it will not only be less expensive, but easier to maintain, and greatly simplify your life.

35. **Consider a smaller car**. This is a big move, but if you have a large car or SUV, you may not really need something that big. It's more expensive, uses more gas, harder to maintain, harder to park. Simplify your life with less car. You don't need to go tiny, especially if you have a family, but try to find as small a car as can fit you or your family comfortably. Maybe not something you're going to do today, but something to think about over the long term.

36. **Learn what "enough" is**. Our materialistic society today is about getting more and more, with no end in sight. Sure, you can get the latest gadget, and more clothes and shoes. More stuff. But when will you have enough? Most people don't know, and thus they keep buying more. It's a never ending cycle. Get off the cycle by figuring out how much is enough. And then stop when you get there.

37. **Create a simple weekly dinner menu**. If figuring out what's for dinner is a nightly stressor for you or your family, consider creating a weekly menu. Decide on a week's worth of simple dinners, set a specific dinner for each night of the week, go grocery shopping for the ingredients. Now you know what's for dinner each night, and you have all the ingredients necessary. No need for difficult recipes — find ones that can be done

in 10-15 minutes (or less).

38. Eat healthy. It might not be obvious how eating healthy relates to simplicity, but think about the opposite: if you eat fatty, greasy, salty, sugary, fried foods all the time, you are sure to have higher medical needs over the long term. We could be talking years from now, but imagine frequent doctor visits, hospitalization, going to the pharmacist, getting therapy, having surgery, taking insulin shots ... you get the idea. Being unhealthy is complicated. Eating healthy simplifies all of that greatly, over the long term.

39. Exercise. This goes along the same lines as eating healthy, as it simplifies your life in the long run, but it goes even further: exercise helps burn off stress and makes you feel better. It's great.

40. Declutter before organizing. Many people make the mistake of taking a cluttered desk or filing cabinet or closet or drawer, and trying to organize it. Unfortunately, that's not only hard to do, it keeps things complicated. Simplify the process by getting rid of as much of the junk as possible, and then organizing. If you declutter enough, you won't need to organize at all.

41. Have a place for everything. Age-old advice, but it's the best advice on keeping things organized. After you declutter.

42. Find inner simplicity. I'm not much of a spiritual person, but I have found that spending a little time with my inner self creates a peaceful simplicity rather

43

than a chaotic confusion. This could be time praying or communing with God, or time spent meditating or journaling or getting to know yourself, or time spent in nature. However you do it, working on your inner self is worth the time.

43. **Learn to decompress from stress**. Every life is filled with stress — no matter how much you simplify your life, you'll still have stress (except in the case of the ultimate simplifier, death). So after you go through stress, find ways to decompress.

44. **Try living without a car**. OK, this isn't something I've done, but many others have. It's something I would do if I didn't have kids. Walk, bike, or take public transportation. It reduces expenses and gives you time to think. A car is also very complicating, needing not only car payments, but insurance, registration, safety inspections, maintenance, repairs, gas and more.

45. **Find a creative outlet for self-expression**. Whether that's writing, poetry, painting, drawing, creating movies, designing websites, dance, skateboarding, whatever. We have a need for self-expression, and finding a way to do that makes your life much more fulfilling. Allow this to replace much of the busy-work you're eliminating from your life.

46. **Simplify your goals**. Instead of having half a dozen goals or more, simplify it to one goal. Not only will this make you less stressed, it will make you more successful. You'll be able to focus on that One Goal, and give it all of your energy. That gives you much better chances for success.

47. Single-task. Multi-tasking is more complicated, more stressful, and generally less productive. Instead, do one task at a time.

48. Simplify your filing system. Stacking a bunch of papers just doesn't work. But a filing system doesn't have to be complicated to be useful. Create a simple system.

49. Develop equanimity. If every little thing that happens to you sends you into anger or stress, your life might never be simple. Learn to detach yourself, and be more at peace.

50. Reduce your consumption of advertising. Advertising makes us want things. That's what it's designed to do, and it works. Find ways to reduce your exposure to advertising, whether that's in print, online, broadcast, or elsewhere. You'll want much less.

51. Live life more deliberately. Do every task slowly, with ease, paying full attention to what you're doing.

52. Make a Most Important Tasks (MITs) list each day. Set just 3 very important things you want to accomplish each day. Don't start with a long list of things you probably won't get done by the end of the day. A simple list of 3 things, ones that would make you feel like you accomplished something.

53. Create morning and evening routines. A great way to simplify your life is to create routines at the start and end of your day.

54. Create a morning writing ritual. If you enjoy

writing, like I do, make it a peaceful, productive ritual.

55. **Learn to do nothing**. Doing nothing can be an art form, and it should be a part of every life.

56. **Read Walden, by Thoreau**. The quintessential text on simplifying. Available on Wikisources for free.

57. **Go for quality, not quantity**. Try not to have a ton of stuff in your life ... instead, have just a few possessions, but ones that you really love, and that will last for a long time.

58. **Read Simplify Your Life, by Elaine St. James**. One of my favorite all-time authors on simplicity.

59. **Fill your day with simple pleasures**. Make a list of your favorite simple pleasures, and sprinkle them throughout your day.

60. **Simplify your RSS feeds**. If you've got dozens of feeds, or more than a hundred (as I once did), you probably have a lot of stress in trying to keep up with them all. Simplify your feed reading.

61. **But subscribe to Unclutterer**. Probably the best blog on simplifying your stuff and routines (along with Zen Habits, of course!).

62. **Create an easy-to-maintain yard**.

63. **Carry less stuff**. Are your pockets bulging? Consider carrying only the essentials.

64. **Simplify your online life**.

65. **Strive to automate your income**. This isn't the easiest task, but it can (and has) been done. I've been working towards it myself.

66. **Simplify your budget**. Many people skip budgeting (which is very important) because it's too hard or too complicated.

67. **Simplify your financial life**.

68. **Learn to pack light**. Who wants to lug a bunch of luggage around on a trip?

69. **Use a minimalist productivity system**. The minimal Zen To Done is all you need. Everything else is icing.

70. **Leave space around things in your day**. Whether they're appointments, or things you need to do, don't stack them back-to-back. Leave a little space between things you need to do, so you will have room for contingencies, and you'll go through your day much more relaxed.

71. **Live closer to work**. This might mean getting a job closer to your home, or moving to a home closer to your work. Either will do much to simplify your life.

72. **Always ask: Will this simplify my life?** If the answer is no, reconsider.

Chapter 9:
Eat Slower

One of the problems in our daily lives is that many of us rush through the day, with no time for anything ... and when we have time to get a bite to eat, we gobble it down.

That leads to stressful, unhealthy living.

And with the simple but powerful act of eating slower, we can begin to reverse that lifestyle immediately. How hard is it? You take smaller bites, you chew each bite slower and longer, and you enjoy your meal longer.

It takes a few minutes extra each meal, and yet it can have profound effects.

You may have already heard of the Slow Food Movement, started in Italy almost two decades ago to counter the fast food movement. Everything that fast food is, Slow Food isn't.

If you read the Slow Food Manifesto, you'll see that it's not just about health — it's about a lifestyle. And whether you want to adopt that lifestyle or not, there are some reasons you should consider the simple act of eating slower:

1. **Lose weight**. A growing number of studies confirm that just by eating slower, you'll consume fewer calories — in fact, enough to lose 20 pounds a year without doing anything different or eating anything different. The reason is that it takes about minutes for

our brains to register that we're full. If we eat fast, we can continue eating past the point where we're full. If we eat slowly, we have time to realize we're full, and stop on time. Now, I would still recommend that you eat healthier foods, but if you're looking to lose weight, eating slowly should be a part of your new lifestyle.

2. **Enjoy your food**. This reason is just as powerful, in my opinion. It's hard to enjoy your food if it goes by too quickly. In fact, I think it's fine to eat sinful foods, if you eat a small amount slowly. Think about it: you want to eat sinful foods (desserts, fried foods, pizza, etc.) because they taste good. But if you eat them fast, what's the point? If you eat them slowly, you can get the same amount of great taste, but with less going into your stomach. That's math that works for me. And that argument aside, I think you are just happier by tasting great food and enjoying it fully, by eating slowly. Make your meals a gastronomic pleasure, not a thing you do rushed, between stressful events.

3. **Better digestion**. If you eat slower, you'll chew your food better, which leads to better digestion. Digestion actually starts in the mouth, so the more work you do up there, the less you'll have to do in your stomach. This can help lead to fewer digestive problems.

4. **Less stress**. Eating slowly, and paying attention to our eating, can be a great form of mindfulness exercise. Be in the moment, rather than rushing through a meal thinking about what you need to do next. When you eat, you should eat. This kind of mindfulness, I believe, will lead to a less stressful life, and long-term happiness. Give it a try.

5. **Rebel against fast food and fast life**. Our hectic, fast-paced, stressful, chaotic lives — the Fast Life — leads to eating Fast Food, and eating it quickly. This is a lifestyle that is dehumanizing us, making us unhealthy, stressed out, and unhappy. We rush through our day, doing one mindless task after another, without taking the time to live life, to enjoy life, to relate to each other, to be human. That's not a good thing in my book. Instead, rebel against that entire lifestyle and philosophy...with the small act of eating slower. Don't eat Fast Food. Eat at a good restaurant, or better yet, cook your own food and enjoy it fully. Taste life itself.

Section 2:

Productivity

Chapter 10:
Purpose Your Day: Most Important Tasks

I've mentioned this briefly in my morning routine, but I thought I'd explain a little bit more about MITs - Most Important Tasks. It's not an original concept, but one that I use on a daily basis and that has helped me out tremendously.

It's very simple: your MIT is the task you most want or need to get done today. In my case, I've tweaked it a bit so that I have three MITs — the three things I must accomplish today. Do I get a lot more done than three things? Of course. But the idea is that no matter what else I do today, these are the things I want to be sure of doing. So, the MIT is the first thing I do each day, right after I have a glass of water to wake me up.

And here's the key to the MITs for me: at least one of the MITs should be related to one of my goals. While the other two can be work stuff (and usually are), one must be a goal next-action. This ensures that I am doing something to move my goals forward that day.

And that makes all the difference in the world. Each day, I've done something to make my dreams come true. It's built into my morning routine: set a next-action to accomplish for one of my goals. And so it happens each day, automatically.

Another key: do your MITs first thing in the morning, either at home or when you first get to work. If you put them off to later, you will get busy and run out of time to do them. Get them out of the way, and the rest of the day is gravy!

It's such a small thing to implement, and yet I'm raving about it like it's a huge revelation. But it is. Sometimes small things can make big differences. I highly recommend you give it a go.

Chapter 11:
Focus on the Big Rocks

If your week is seven buckets, and you go into each bucket without planning ahead, and you fill it up with little pebbles and grains of sand and whatever other debris comes your way ... soon there will be no room for the Big Rocks. Your buckets fill up faster than you know it, and once your buckets are full, you're done. You can't get bigger buckets.

What you can do is put the Big Rocks in first, and fill in the pebbles and sand around them.

The Big Rocks are the major things you want to get done this week. A report, launching a new website, going to the gym, spending time with your spouse and kids, achieving your dreams. These Big Rocks get pushed back from week to week because we never have time to do them — our days fill up too quickly, and before we know it, weeks have passed and the Big Rocks are still sitting on the side, untouched.

Plan your week ahead of time, placing your Big Rocks first.

This is a similar concept to MITs, except on a weekly scale instead of a daily scale. Big Rocks are your MITs for the week.

Here's how you do it (with the unavoidable list, of course!):

1. **Make a list**. At the beginning of the week — Sunday evening or Monday morning — write out the Big Rocks that you want to accomplish this week. These should be the important things — if you looked back on the week and said you did them, you would be proud of having done them. Be sure to include not only work stuff, but some of the tasks that will further along your life's goals and dreams.

2. **Keep it short**. In the beginning, just have 4-6 ... you don't need to try to do 10 or more Big Rocks, especially not at first. Later, you may get better at judging how many Big Rocks you can do in a week, but for now, shoot for about one per day.

3. **Place the Rocks**. Look at your weekly schedule. If you don't have one, write out the days of the week with one-hour blocks (or print out a schedule from an online calendar). Write out pre-existing appointments. Now take your Big Rocks, and put them in the schedule. Try to put them in a spot where you know you'll get them done. Not a spot that's traditionally too busy to concentrate, and not in a little half-hour window between meetings. Give yourself time to do it.

4. **Leave space for the incoming pebbles**. Don't fill in the rest of the schedule if possible. Every morning, look at your schedule and commit yourself to doing the Big Rock(s) for that day. That's your MIT for the day. If there are less important MITs, you can put them in the schedule, but don't put too much. A tight schedule tends to bump into itself, pushing things back when other things inevitably take too long.

5. **Do it early**. If you can, place your Big Rocks first thing in the morning. Don't schedule them for later in the day if possible, because by that time, a few fires have come up, and the Big Rock will get pushed back as always. Do it first, and then you've got the rest of the day for the busy-work.

6. **Be Proud**. When your week's done, look back on it — if you got any (or all!) of the Big Rocks done, be proud of yourself and happy. It feels good! How does this simple method make you more productive? Well, productivity isn't about doing a lot of stuff. It's about getting the important stuff done. But if you're running around doing all the little stuff ... sure, you did a lot and you were very busy, but how much did you really accomplish? Oftentimes we can look back on our week and say, "I didn't get a lot done, but I sure was stressed doing it!"

This is a way of getting the important stuff done. Sure, you'll still have to worry about the little stuff. But at the end of the week, you can look back and say that you've been productive. It makes a world of difference.

Chapter 12:
Clear Out Your Inbox

I use Gmail exclusively for email, and it constitutes a major part of my two day jobs. I get a fair amount of email each hour, and I am pretty quick at responding.

However, one thing you'll notice about my Gmail inbox is that it is just about always empty.

It gives me a Zen feeling to have a clean inbox, a feeling of peace and calm and satisfaction. I highly recommend it to everyone. I wasn't always like this — I had many emails in my inbox in the past. They would sit in there, sometimes unread, sometimes just waiting on an action, sometimes waiting to be filed, and others just waiting because I was procrastinating. I also had many folders for filing my email, so I could find them when I needed them. It would take me awhile to file sometimes, so I would put it off. Many people I know are the same way.

But GTD changed that (as well as 43 Folders and others), and for nearly a year now, I've been fairly consistent about having a clean inbox.

Here are my simple steps to achieving Email Zen:

1. **Don't check email first thing in the morning, or have it constantly on**. This is a tip offered by many blogs, so nothing new here. Checking email first thing will get you stuck in email for awhile. Instead, do your most important thing for the day, or the thing you've been procrastinating on the most. Then check email.

Better yet, do 2 or 3 things first. Also, if you are constantly checking email throughout the day, or it notifies you as soon as an email comes in, you will be constantly distracted and not able to focus on the task before you. I check once an hour, but you might have different needs.

2. **When you check your email, dispose of each one, one at a time, right away**. Make a decision on what needs to be done on each email.

   2a. **Is it junk or some forwarded email?** Trash it immediately.

   2b. **Is it a long email that you just need to read for information?** File it in a Read folder (or tag it Read and archive) or print it to read on the road (while waiting in line, for example).

   2c. **If the email requires action, make a note of the action on your to-do or GTD lists to do later**. Also note to check the email for info if necessary. Then archive the email. You can easily find it later when you need to do that task.

   2d. **If you can respond to it in a minute or two, do so immediately**. Don't put it off. If you wait, you'll end up with a backlog of emails to respond to, and you may never get around to it. I respond quickly, with a short note, and send it right away. That way I'm viewed as responsive and on top of things.

   2e. If you need to follow up on the email later, or are waiting for a response, note it on a Waiting For list. Don't just leave it in your inbox as a reminder.

3. **I have only one folder: Archive**. When I respond to an email, or finish reading it if it doesn't need response, or note it on my to-do list, I archive it. Simple as that. You could add a Read folder if you want. I usually print longer ones to read later, like during lunch or while waiting for something. Other people have an Action folder or a Waiting For folder, but I find that that's just an additional inbox (or "bucket" as GTD's David Allen calls it) that you have to constantly check. I don't like to check extra folders. I have my to-do lists and my Waiting For list, and that's good enough. So it's as simple as pressing "Archive" on an email, and if I need to find it later, Gmail's search is so good that it's easy to find. I've never had any problems with this system.

Email Zen is that easy: check email at regular periods, take action on each email right away (or note it on a list to do later) and archive.

Ahhh. Empty inbox!

Chapter 13:
Clear Your Desk

Once upon a time, my desk was cluttered with all the things I was currently working on — not to mention dozens of things I wasn't working on: notes, post-its, phone numbers, papers to be filed, stacks of stuff to work on later. I was too busy to organize it, and if I ever did get it cleared, it would pile up soon after.

It's a different story today. These days, my desk is always clear, except for the one thing I'm working on, and perhaps a notebook and pen for jotting down notes, ideas or to-dos as they come up. It's a liberating feeling ... it calms me ... it reduces stress and chaos ... it definitely makes things easier to find ... and it makes me more efficient and productive.

How did I make the transformation? Well, it wasn't an easy journey, and I've improved over the years, but the basic steps are outlined below. The important thing to remember is that you must have a system in place, and you must teach yourself to follow the system. Otherwise, you just clean your desk, and it gets messy again.

Here's the system:

1. **First, take everything on your desk and in your drawers, and put them in one big pile**. Put it in your "in basket" (if it doesn't fit, pile it next to your desk or something). From now on, everything that comes in must go in your in basket, and you process everything as below.

2. **Process this pile from the top down**. Never re-sort, never skip a single piece of paper, never put a piece of paper back on the pile. Do what needs to be done with that paper, and then move on to the next in the pile. The options: trash it, delegate it, file it, do it, or put it on a list to do later. In that order of preference. Do it if it takes 2 minutes or less to complete. If it takes more, and you can't trash, delegate or file it, then put it on a list of to-dos (more on your to-do list in another post).

3. **Repeat at least once daily to keep desk clear**. The end of the day is best, but I tend to process and tidy up as I go through the day. Once you've processed your pile, your desk is clear. You've trashed or filed or somehow put everything where it belongs (not on top of your desk or stashed in a drawer). Keep it that way. You must follow the system above: put everything in your inbox, then take action on each piece of paper in the inbox with one of the steps listed. If an item is on your to-do list, you can keep the paper associated with it in an "Action" folder. But you must regularly (daily or weekly) go through this folder to ensure that everything is purged.

It's that simple. Have a phone number on a post-it? Don't leave it on top of your desk. File it in your rolodex or contacts program. Have something you need to work on later? Don't keep the papers on top of your desk. Put it on your to-do list, and file the papers in your Action folder. File or trash or delegate everything else.

Leaving stuff on top of your desk is procrastination (and as a procrastinator, I should know). If you put it off until later, things will be sure to pile up on your desk. Deal with them immediately, make a decision, take action.

What I've described is a good habit to learn, but it takes time to learn it. You'll slip. Just remind yourself, and then do it. Soon it'll be a habit you have a hard time breaking. And trust me, once you're used to your desk being clear, you won't want to break this habit.

Chapter 14:
Become an Early Riser

"Early to bed and early to rise makes a man healthy, wealthy and wise." - Ben Franklin, famously

"Put no trust in the benefits to accrue from early rising, as set forth by the infatuated Franklin..."
- Mark Twain

Recently, reader Rob asked me about my habit of waking at 4:30 a.m. each day, and asked me to write about the health benefits of rising early, which I thought was an excellent question. Unfortunately, there are none, that I know of.

However, there are a ton of other great benefits.

Now, let me first say that if you are a night owl, and that works for you, I think that's great. There's no reason to change, especially if you're happy with it. But for me, switching from being a night owl to an early riser (and yes, it is possible) has been a godsend. It has helped me in so many ways that I'd never go back. Here are just a few:

1. **Greet the day**. I love being able to get up, and greet a wonderful new day. I suggest creating a morning ritual that includes saying thanks for your blessings. I'm inspired by the Dalai Lama, who said, " Everyday, think as you wake up, 'today I am fortunate to have woken up, I am alive, I have a precious human life, I am not going to waste it. I am going to use all my energies to develop myself, to expand my heart out to

69

others, to achieve enlightenment for the benefit of all beings, I am going to have kind thoughts towards others, I am not going to get angry or think badly about others, I am going to benefit others as much as I can.' "

2. **Amazing start**. I used to start my day by jumping out of bed, late as usual, and rushing to get myself and the kids ready, and rushing to drop them to school and come in to work late. I would walk into work, looking rumpled and barely awake, grumpy and behind everyone else.

3. **Not a great start to your day**. Now, I have a renewing morning ritual, I've gotten so much done before 8 a.m., my kids are early and so am I, and by the time everyone else gets in to work, I've already gotten a head start. There is no better way to start off your day than to wake early, in my experience.

4. **Quietude**. No kids yelling, no babies crying, no soccer balls, no cars, no television noise. The early morning hours are so peaceful, so quiet. It's my favorite time of day. I truly enjoy that time of peace, that time to myself, when I can think, when I can read, when I can breathe.

5. **Sunrise**. People who wake late miss one of the greatest feats of nature, repeated in full stereovision each and every day — the rise of the sun. I love how the day slowly gets brighter, when the midnight blue turns to lighter blue, when the brilliant colors start to seep into the sky, when nature is painted in incredible colors. I like doing my early morning run during this time, and I look up at the sky as I run and say to the

world, "What a glorious day!" Really. I really do that. Corny, I know.

6. **Breakfast**. Rise early and you actually have time for breakfast. I'm told it's one of the most important meals of the day. Without breakfast, your body is running on fumes until you are so hungry at lunchtime that you eat whatever unhealthy thing you can find. The fattier and sugarier, the betterier. But eat breakfast, and you are sated until later. Plus, eating breakfast while reading my book and drinking my coffee in the quiet of the morning is eminently more enjoyable than scarfing something down on the way to work, or at your desk.

7. **Exercise**. There are other times to exercise besides the early morning, of course, but I've found that while exercising right after work is also very enjoyable, it's also liable to be canceled because of other things that come up. Morning exercise is virtually never canceled.

8. **Productivity**. Mornings, for me at least, are the most productive time of day. I like to do some writing in the morning, when there are no distractions, before I check my email or blog stats. I get so much more done by starting on my work in the morning. Then, when evening rolls around, I have no work that I need to do, and I can spend it with family.

9. **Goal time**. Got goals? Well, you should. And there's no better time to review them and plan for them and do your goal tasks than first thing. You should have one goal that you want to accomplish this week. And every morning, you should decide what one thing you can do today to move yourself further towards that goal. And then, if possible, do that first thing in the morning.

10. **Commute**. No one likes rush-hour traffic, except for Big Oil. Commute early, and the traffic is much lighter, and you get to work faster, and thus save yourself more time. Or better yet, commute by bike. (Or even better yet, work from home.)

11. **Appointments**. It's much easier to make those early appointments on time if you get up early. Showing up late for those appointments is a bad signal to the person you're meeting. Showing up early will impress them. Plus, you get time to prepare.

How to Become an Early Riser

- **Don't make drastic changes**. Start slowly, by waking just 15-30 minutes earlier than usual. Get used to this for a few days. Then cut back another 15 minutes. Do this gradually until you get to your goal time.

- **Allow yourself to sleep earlier**. You might be used to staying up late, perhaps watching TV or surfing the Internet. But if you continue this habit, while trying to get up earlier, sooner or later one is going to give. And if it is the early rising that gives, then you will crash and sleep late and have to start over. I suggest going to bed earlier, even if you don't think you'll sleep, and read while in bed. If you're really tired, you just might fall asleep much sooner than you think.

- **Put your alarm clock far from you bed**. If it's right next to your bed, you'll shut it off or hit snooze. Never hit snooze. If it's far from your bed, you have to get up out of bed to shut it off. By then, you're up. Now you just have to stay up.

- **Go out of the bedroom as soon as you shut off the alarm**. Don't allow yourself to rationalize going back to bed. Just force yourself to go out of the room. My habit is to stumble into the bathroom and go pee. By the time I've done that, and flushed the toilet and washed my hands and looked at my ugly mug in the mirror, I'm awake enough to face the day.

- **Do not rationalize**. If you allow your brain to talk you out of getting up early, you'll never do it. Don't make getting back in bed an option.

- **Have a good reason**. Set something to do early in the morning that's important. This reason will motivate you to get up. I like to write in the morning, so that's my reason. Also, when I'm done with that, I like to read all of your comments!

- **Make waking up early a reward**. Yes, it might seem at first that you're forcing yourself to do something hard, but if you make it pleasurable, soon you will look forward to waking up early. A good reward is to make a hot cup of coffee or tea and read a book. Other rewards might be a tasty treat for breakfast (smoothies! yum!) or watching the sunrise, or meditating. Find something that's pleasurable for you, and allow yourself to do it as part of your morning routine.

- **Take advantage of all that extra time**. Don't wake up an hour or two early just to read your blogs, unless that's a major goal of yours. Don't wake up early and waste that extra time. Get a jump start on your day! I like to use that time to get a head start on preparing my kids' lunches, on planning for the rest of the day (when I set my MITs), on exercising or meditating, and on reading. By the time 6:30 rolls around, I've done more than many people do the entire day.

Chapter 15:
Become Motivated When You're in a Slump

Even the most motivated of us — you, me, Tony Robbins — can feel unmotivated at times. In fact, sometimes we get into such a slump that even thinking about making positive changes seems too difficult.

But it's not hopeless: with some small steps, baby ones in fact, you can get started down the road to positive change.

Yes, I know, it seems impossible at times. You don't feel like doing anything. I've been there, and in fact I still feel that way from time to time. You're not alone. But I've learned a few ways to break out of a slump, and we'll take a look at those today.

This was inspired by reader Roy C. Carlson, who asked:

"I was wondering if you could do a piece on why it can be hard for someone to change direction and start taking control of their life. I have to say I'm in this boat and advice on getting out of my slump would be great."

Roy is just one of many with a slump like that. Again, I feel that way sometimes myself, and in fact sometimes I struggle to motivate myself to exercise — and I'll use that as an example of how to break out of the slump.

When I fall out of exercise, due to illness or injury or disruption from things going on in my life, it's hard to get started again. I don't even feel like thinking about it, sometimes. But I've always found a way to break out of that slump, and here are some things I've learned that have helped:

1. **One Goal**. Whenever I've been in a slump, I've discovered that it's often because I have too much going on in my life. I'm trying to do too much. And it saps my energy and motivation. It's probably the most common mistake that people make: they try to take on too much, try to accomplish too many goals at once. You cannot maintain energy and focus (the two most important things in accomplishing a goal) if you are trying to do two or more goals at once. It's not possible — I've tried it many times. You have to choose one goal, for now, and focus on it completely. I know, that's hard. Still, I speak from experience. You can always do your other goals when you've accomplished your One Goal.

2. **Find inspiration**. Inspiration, for me, comes from others who have achieved what I want to achieve, or who are currently doing it. I read other blogs, books, magazines. I Google my goal, and read success stories. Zen Habits is just one place for inspiration, not only from me but from many readers who have achieved amazing things.

3. **Get excited**. This sounds obvious, but most people don't think about it much: if you want to break out of a slump, get yourself excited about a goal. But how can you do that when you don't feel motivated? Well, it starts with inspiration from others (see above), but you have to take that excitement and build on it. For me, I've learned that by talking to my wife about it, and to others, and reading as much about it as possible, and visualizing what it would be like to be successful

(seeing the benefits of the goal in my head), I get excited about a goal. Once I've done that, it's just a matter of carrying that energy forward and keeping it going.

4. **Build anticipation**. This will sound hard, and many people will skip this tip. But it really works. It helped me quit smoking after many failed attempts. If you find inspiration and want to do a goal, don't start right away. Many of us will get excited and want to start today. That's a mistake. Set a date in the future — a week or two, or even a month — and make that your Start Date. Mark it on the calendar. Get excited about that date. Make it the most important date in your life. In the meantime, start writing out a plan. And do some of the steps below. Because by delaying your start, you are building anticipation, and increasing your focus and energy for your goal.

5. **Post your goal**. Print out your goal in big words. Make your goal just a few words long, like a mantra ("Exercise 15 mins. Daily"), and post it up on your wall or refrigerator. Post it at home and work. Put it on your computer desktop. You want to have big reminders about your goal, to keep your focus and keep your excitement going. A picture of your goal (like a model with sexy abs, for example) also helps.

6. **Commit publicly**. None of us likes to look bad in front of others. We will go the extra mile to do something we've said publicly. For example, when I wanted to run my first marathon, I started writing a column about it in my local daily newspaper. The entire island of Guam (pop. 160K) knew about my goal. I couldn't back down, and even though my

motivation came and went, I stuck with it and completed it. Now, you don't have to commit to your goal in your daily newspaper, but you can do it with friends and family and co-workers, and you can do it on your blog if you have one. And hold yourself accountable — don't just commit once, but commit to giving progress updates to everyone every week or so.

7. **Think about it daily**. If you think about your goal every day, it is much more likely to become true. To this end, posting the goal on your wall or computer desktop (as mentioned above) helps a lot. Sending yourself daily reminders also helps. And if you can commit to doing one small thing to further your goal (even just 5 minutes) every single day, your goal will almost certainly come true.

8. **Get support**. It's hard to accomplish something alone. When I decided to run my marathon, I had the help of friends and family, and I had a great running community on Guam who encouraged me at 5K races and did long runs with me. When I decided to quit smoking, I joined an online forum and that helped tremendously. And of course, my wife Eva helped every step of the way. I couldn't have done these goals without her, or without the others who supported me. Find your support network, either in the real world or online, or both.

9. **Realize that there's an ebb and flow**. Motivation is not a constant thing that is always there for you. It comes and goes, and comes and goes again, like the tide. But realize that while it may go away, it doesn't do so permanently. It will come back. Just stick it out and wait for that motivation to come back. In the

meantime, read about your goal (see below), ask for help (see below), and do some of the other things listed here until your motivation comes back.

10. **Stick with it**. Whatever you do, don't give up. Even if you aren't feeling any motivation today, or this week, don't give up. Again, that motivation will come back. Think of your goal as a long journey, and your slump is just a little bump in the road. You can't give up with every little bump. Stay with it for the long term, ride out the ebbs and surf on the flows, and you'll get there.

11. **Start small**. Really small. If you are having a hard time getting started, it may be because you're thinking too big. If you want to exercise, for example, you may be thinking that you have to do these intense workouts 5 days a week. No — instead, do small, tiny, baby steps. Just do 2 minutes of exercise. I know, that sounds wimpy. But it works. Commit to 2 minutes of exercise for one week. You may want to do more, but just stick to 2 minutes. It's so easy, you can't fail. Do it at the same time, every day. Just some crunches, 2 pushups, and some jogging in place. Once you've done 2 minutes a day for a week, increase it to 5, and stick with that for a week. In a month, you'll be doing 15-20. Want to wake up early? Don't think about waking at 5 a.m. Instead, think about waking 10 minutes earlier for a week. That's all. Once you've done that, wake 10 minutes earlier than that. Baby steps.

12. **Build on small successes**. Again, if you start small for a week, you're going to be successful. You can't fail if you start with something ridiculously easy. Who can't exercise for 2 minutes? (If that's you, I apologize.) And you'll feel successful, and good about yourself.

Take that successful feeling and build on it, with another baby step. Add 2-3 minutes to your exercise routine, for example. With each step (and each step should last about a week), you will feel even more successful. Make each step really, really small, and you won't fail. After a couple of months, your tiny steps will add up to a lot of progress and a lot of success.

13. **Read about it daily**. When I lose motivation, I just read a book or blog about my goal. It inspires me and reinvigorates me. For some reason, reading helps motivate and focus you on whatever you're reading about. So read about your goal every day, if you can, especially when you're not feeling motivated.

14. **Call for help when your motivation ebbs**. Having trouble? Ask for help. Email me. Join an online forum. Get a partner to join you. Call your mom. It doesn't matter who, just tell them your problems, and talking about it will help. Ask them for advice. Ask them to help you overcome your slump. It works.

15. **Think about the benefits, not the difficulties**. One common problem is that we think about how hard something is. Exercise sounds so hard! Just thinking about it makes you tired. But instead of thinking about how hard something is, think about what you will get out of it. For example, instead of thinking about how tiring exercise can be, focus on how good you'll feel when you're done, and how you'll be healthier and slimmer over the long run. The benefits of something will help energize you.

16. **Squash negative thoughts; replace them with positive ones.** Along those lines, it's important to start monitoring your thoughts. Recognize negative self-talk, which is really what's causing your slump. Just spend a few days becoming aware of every negative thought. Then, after a few days, try squashing those negative thoughts like a bug, and then replacing them with a corresponding positive thought. Squash, "This is too hard!" and replace it with, "I can do this! If that wimp Leo can do it, so can I!" It sounds corny, but it works. Really..

Chapter 16:
Make the Most of Your Laziest Days

Ever have one of those unproductive days when you just feel lazy, and don't want to work on anything on your to-do list?

We all have our lazy and unproductive days. Sometimes we didn't get enough sleep, sometimes we just don't have motivation, and sometimes we get distracted by a fun new game (mine yesterday was befuddlr).

So what do you do? Today, we'll look at some of my favorite unproductivity-day strategies.

Reader Ben Helps recently asked:

"Do you go through cycles of increased and decreased productivity?"

It seems that whatever I try to manage the myriad things I have to keep track of and get done (running my own businesses), I have weeks where I'm on top of it all and feeling great. Unfortunately I also have weeks where I feel like I'm letting lots of things slide and not achieving much.

Great question, Ben! Quick answer: I totally, totally have cycles of increased and decreased production! I hope I don't convey the wrong idea, that I'm productive all the time.

I think, for me, it's a matter of finding ways to still get the important stuff done when I'm not feeling productive, and also allowing myself to take breaks now and then. Our minds need a break — we can't go full charge all the time.

Here are my most favoritest ways of making the most of an unproductivity-filled day:

1. **Find something fun to do**. If you're feeling unmotivated, it may just be that the things on your to-do list bore you. You need to find something exciting to do! This can be a bit of a challenge for some, but here's how to do it: take a step back, close your eyes, and just let your mind go. What would be fun to do today? How can you get outside of your normal routine? What are you passionate about? What would be fresh and new to you? Let the ideas flow, then start writing them down (you can open your eyes at this point). Then choose something fun and exciting from your list, even if it's not something urgent — it's better than doing nothing!

   Getting excited about something is the best way to get out of those unmotivated doldrums. Find your passion, and pursue it!

2. **Kill distractions**. What is it that's distracting you today? Whether that's some new website you discovered (Zen Habits?), a forum, Digg, some form of solitaire or Bejeweled, or whatever ...   if you find a way to block yourself from that distraction, you can get a lot more done. It's hard, I know. A good method: have a friend or coworker stop you from using the distraction. Another good method: disconnect the Internet. I know I get a lot more done

when I do that. :)

3. **Put something dreadful at the top of my list**. If there's something that I've been putting off for awhile, something that put fear into my heart, I put that at the top of my list for today, and put a bunch of other things I need to do below that. Guess what? I might not do the thing at the top of my list. But in order to procrastinate on that dreaded item, I crank through a bunch of other things on my list. That's productive unproductivity for you!

4. **Just relax**. OK, so you don't get anything done today. Does the world end? Sometimes, especially if you've been doing a lot of work, your brain just needs a rest. Take that rest day! Let yourself rejuvenate. If you can take the day off, do it! If not, just goof around today, and get back to work tomorrow. You might just find yourself recharged.

5. **Take a walk**. Sometimes you just need to get the blood circulating. Sitting at your desk all day can take a lot out of you. Get up, walk around, go outside if you can. Ten minutes of fresh air can get you relaxed and ready to crank out the work!

6. **Take a shower**. If you work at home (like I sometimes do), it's very tempting to just get up and start working in your pajamas (or worse). But if you don't feel clean, you might not feel productive. So go take a shower! You'll feel much better, and ready to work. It's amazing how much of a difference a shower and a shave can make!

7. **Take a nap**. The ultimate unproductivity tool. If I can sneak in a nap, it always helps me out. I feel refreshed and much more ready to face the work in front of me. Some great tips from Ririan Project.

8. **Crank up the music**. Nothing gets you going better than an upbeat tune. Seriously, give it a try. Anything that's got a good beat will do. Here's my current playlist of oldies, guaranteed to get you moving (money back if it doesn't work!):

Tommy James and The Shondells - Hanky Panky
Ronettes - Be My Baby
Sam Cooke - Don't Know Much About History
Frankie Valley - Stay (Just A Little Bit Longer)
Diana Ross and The Supremes - Baby Love
Sam Cooke - Stand By Me
Diana Ross and The Supremes - You Can't Hurry
Love The Temptations - My Girl
The Temptations - Just My Imagination
Dusty Springfield - I Only Want To Be With You
Dusty Springfield - Son of a Preacher Man
Frankie Vallie and The Four Seasons - Walk Like A
Man Beatles - Can't Buy Me Love
Kinks - What I Like About You
Kinks - Come Dancing
The Staples Singers - Let's Do It Again

Chapter 17:
Decompress After High Stress

Just like everyone else, I have crazy days that are jam-packed with activity, meetings, people stopping in to see me, hundreds of emails, phone calls and messages, one project after another.

I am usually able to maintain calm and focus in the midst of a workday, but those crazy days can

put my abilities to the test. I stay calm, but the stress levels are definitely higher than I care for.

After all that, I need to decompress.

I have a number of tried-and-true methods that work for me, and I have to say, when I do them, my stress levels drop dramatically.

Here's what works for me:

1. **Deep breathing**. Take a deep breath. Hold it. Now let it out ... slowly. Try counting to 10 as you let out your breath. Feel the tension and stress flowing out of you with your breath. Repeat 3-10 times, as necessary.

2. **Self-massage**. I like to massage my shoulders, neck, head, lower back. It helps a lot. Even better: get your honey to do it for you! Another great relaxation technique is to tense up and then relax each muscle in your body, one at a time, starting from your toes up to your head.

3. **Take a walk**. When I'm in the middle of stress, I like to take 5, and take a walk around the building. I also

do the deep breathing and self-massage mentioned above as I do so. It's a great way of letting go of tension and allowing yourself to re-focus.

4. **Exercise**. This morning, I went to the beach at 5:30 a.m. and went for a swim. It was beautiful at the beach at around sunrise, and the swim was invigorating. Yesterday I went for a bike ride, and the morning before it was a short but refreshing run. Tomorrow I think I'll do another short run. It really gets the stress out of your system and gives you some quiet time to think when you exercise.

5. **Get outdoors**. Even if I didn't do the swim, just being there at the beach, with my decaf coffee (I quit caffeine, remember?), was calming. It's nice to connect with nature and take in the beauty around you. While you're there, stretch, yawn, take some deep breaths, and enjoy.

6. **Sex**. One of the all-time greats. It works like a charm. Seriously. It's probably the best on the list. (Sorry, mom.)

7. **Take a day off**. That's what I'm doing today. Perhaps my favorite thing to do is play hooky. I have lots of vacation and sick leave saved up, so it's not a problem, actually. I'm just going to veg out and allow myself to calm down and center.

8. **Meditate**. You don't need to be trained to have a short, relaxing meditation session. Just sit somewhere quiet, close your eyes, relax, and focus on your breathing. Try to concentrate on it coming into your body, and then going out. When other things pop into your head (they will, inevitably), just acknowledge them (don't try to force them out) and allow them to

leave, and then focus again on your breathing. Do this for as long as you can, and then take a couple of cleansing breaths, and get up a new person.

9. **Read**. I like to throw myself on the couch with a good book. Well, not necessarily a good book — a page-turner. Something that will engross me completely, take my mind off everything else. John Grisham works well for me, as does William Gibson. And Terry Pratchett. Or Ann Patchett, for that matter. And Stephen King. Just get lost in their world.

10. **Love**. I like to spend time with my kids or my wife. Just snuggle with them, focus on them, forget about the world. They are all that's important, and sometimes I need that reminder.

11. **Disconnect**. Turn off the phones, turn off the computer, and shut off the outside world for a little while. These things just raise your stress level. Go offline and forget about the online world! You can do it! Except for Zen Habits. That's the only blog you're allowed to read when you decompress.

12. **Take a nap**. One of my favorites. Just take a 30-minute nap, and you're re-set! A nap is like a restart button for life.

Section 3:
Happiness

Chapter 18:
Cultivate Compassion in Your Life

"If you want others to be happy, practice compassion. If you want to be happy, practice compassion." - Dalai Lama

"My message is the practice of compassion, love and kindness. These things are very useful in our daily life, and also for the whole of human society these practices can be very important." - Dalai Lama

I believe compassion to be one of the few things we can practice that will bring immediate and long-term happiness to our lives. I'm not talking about the short-term gratification of pleasures like sex, drugs or gambling (though I'm not knocking them), but something that will bring true and lasting happiness. The kind that sticks.

The key to developing compassion in your life is to make it a daily practice.

Meditate upon it in the morning (you can do it while checking email), think about it when you interact with others, and reflect on it at night. In this way, it becomes a part of your life. Or as the Dalai Lama also said,

"This is my simple religion. There is no need for temples; no need for complicated philosophy. Our own brain, our own heart is our temple; the philosophy is kindness."

Definition

Let's use the Wikipedia definition of Compassion:

"Compassion is an emotion that is a sense of shared suffering, most often combined with a desire to alleviate or reduce the suffering of another; to show special kindness to those who suffer. Compassion essentially arises through empathy, and is often characterized through actions, wherein a person acting with compassion will seek to aid those they feel compassionate for.

"Compassionate acts are generally considered those which take into account the suffering of others and attempt to alleviate that suffering as if it were one's own. In this sense, the various forms of the Golden Rule are clearly based on the concept of compassion.

"Compassion differs from other forms of helpful or humane behavior in that its focus is primarily on the alleviation of suffering."

Benefits

Why develop compassion in your life? Well, there are scientific studies that suggest there are physical benefits to practicing compassion — people who practice it produce 100 percent more DHEA, which is a hormone that counteracts the aging process, and 23 percent less cortisol — the "stress hormone."

But there are other benefits as well, and these are emotional and spiritual. The main benefit is that it helps you to be more happy, and brings others around you to be more happy. If we agree that it is a common aim of each of us to strive to be happy, then compassion is one of the main tools for achieving that happiness. It is therefore of utmost importance that we cultivate compassion in our lives and practice compassion every day.

How do we do that? This guide contains 7 different practices that you can try out and perhaps incorporate into your every day life.

7 Compassion Practices

1. **Morning ritual**. Greet each morning with a ritual. Try this one, suggest by the Dalai Lama: "Today I am fortunate to have woken up, I am alive, I have a precious human life, I am not going to waste it. I am going to use all my energies to develop myself, to expand my heart out to others, to achieve enlightenment for the benefit of all beings, I am going to have kind thoughts towards others, I am not going to get angry or think badly about others, I am going to benefit others as much as I can." Then, when you've done this, try one of the practices below.

2. **Empathy Practice**. The first step in cultivating compassion is to develop empathy for your fellow human beings. Many of us believe that we have empathy, and on some level nearly all of us do. But many times we are centered on ourselves (I'm no exception) and we let our sense of empathy get rusty. Try this practice: Imagine that a loved one is suffering. Something terrible has happened to him or her. Now try to imagine the pain they are going through. Imagine the suffering in as much detail as possible. After doing this practice for a couple of weeks, you should try moving on to imagining the suffering of others you know, not just those who are close to you.

3. **Commonalities practice**. Instead of recognizing the differences between yourself and others, try to recognize what you have in common. At the root of it all, we are all human beings. We need food, and shelter, and love. We crave attention, and recognition, and affection, and above all, happiness. Reflect on these commonalities you have with every other human being, and ignore the differences. One of my favorite exercises comes from a great article from Ode Magazine — it's a five-step exercise to try when you meet friends and strangers. Do it discreetly and try to do all the steps with the same person. With your attention geared to the other person, tell yourself:

Step 1: "Just like me, this person is seeking happiness in his/her life."

Step 2: "Just like me, this person is trying to avoid suffering in his/her life."

Step 3: "Just like me, this person has known sadness, loneliness and despair."

Step 4: "Just like me, this person is seeking to fill his/her needs."

Step 5: "Just like me, this person is learning about life."

4. **Relief of suffering practice**. Once you can empathize with another person, and understand his humanity and suffering, the next step is to want that person to be free from suffering. This is the heart of compassion — actually the definition of it. Try this exercise: Imagine the suffering of a human being you've met recently. Now imagine that you are the one going through that suffering. Reflect on how much you would like that suffering to end. Reflect on how happy you would be if another human being desired your suffering to end, and acted upon it. Open your heart to that human being and if you feel even a little that you'd want their suffering to end, reflect on that feeling. That's the feeling that you want to develop. With constant practice, that feeling can be grown and nurtured.

5. **Act of kindness practice**. Now that you've gotten good at the 4th practice, take the exercise a step further. Imagine again the suffering of someone you know or met recently. Imagine again that you are that person, and are going through that suffering. Now imagine that another human being would like your suffering to end — perhaps your mother or another loved one. What would you like for that person to do to end your suffering? Now reverse roles: you are the person who desires for the other person's suffering to end. Imagine that you do something to help ease the suffering, or end it completely.

96

Once you get good at this stage, practice doing something small each day to help end the suffering of others, even in a tiny way. Even a smile, or a kind word, or doing an errand or chore, or just talking about a problem with another person. Practice doing something kind to help ease the suffering of others. When you are good at this, find a way to make it a daily practice, and eventually a throughout-the-day practice.

6. **Those who mistreat us practice**. The final stage in these compassion practices is to not only want to ease the suffering of those we love and meet, but even those who mistreat us. When we encounter someone who mistreats us, instead of acting in anger, withdraw. Later, when you are calm and more detached, reflect on that person who mistreated you. Try to imagine the background of that person. Try to imagine what that person was taught as a child. Try to imagine the day or week that person was going through, and what kind of bad things had happened to that person. Try to imagine the mood and state of mind that person was in — the suffering that person must have been going through to mistreat you that way. And understand that their action was not about you, but about what they were going through.

   Now think some more about the suffering of that poor person, and see if you can imagine trying to stop the suffering of that person. And then reflect that if you mistreated someone, and they acted with kindness and compassion toward you, whether that would make you less likely to mistreat that person the next time, and more likely to be kind to that person. Once you have mastered this practice of reflection, try acting with compassion and understanding the next time a person treats you. Do it in little doses, until you are good at it. Practice makes perfect.

7. **Evening routine**. I highly recommend that you take a few minutes before you go to bed to reflect upon your day. Think about the people you met and talked to, and how you treated each other. Think about your goal that you stated this morning, to act with compassion towards others.

How well did you do? What could you do better? What did you learn from your experiences today? And if you have time, try one of the above practices and exercises.

These compassionate practices can be done anywhere, any time. At work, at home, on the road, while traveling, while at a store, while at the home of a friend or family member. By sandwiching your day with a morning and evening ritual, you can frame your day properly, in an attitude of trying to practice compassion and develop it within yourself. And with practice, you can begin to do it throughout the day, and throughout your lifetime.

This, above all, with bring happiness to your life and to those around you.

Chapter 19:
Escape Materialism

"Happiness is having a large, loving, caring, close-knit family in another city." - George Burns

Money can't buy you love. It can't buy you happiness either.

Today's materialistic world often urges us to buy the coolest gadgets, the trendiest clothes, bigger and better things, but research shows that possessions and purchases don't buy us happiness. According to an article on CNN:

"By and large, money buys happiness only for those who lack the basic needs. Once you pass an income of $50,000, more money doesn't buy much more happiness, [according to a happiness studies]."

So while we are being pushed towards materialism, it's for monetary gain by corporations, not for our own happiness. Unfortunately, it's hard to escape the trap of materialism, and find happiness in other ways than buying stuff online or finding joy in the mall.

But it's possible. Here's a guide to finding a materialism-free life and discovering true happiness.

Escaping Materialism

All around us, there are messages telling us to buy stuff. On the Internet (blogs included), we see continuous advertising trying to get us to purchase a product or service. It's the main reason for television, and movies are continually made with products placed throughout, so that we aren't always sure what is advertising and what was put in there by the director.

Flip on the radio or open up a newspaper or magazine, and you're bombarded my more advertising. Go to a shopping center/mall, and the urge to buy comes from every direction.

This message to continually buy, buy, buy ... and that it will somehow make us happier ... is drilled into our heads from the days of Happy Meals and cartoons until the day we die. It's inescapable.

Well, almost. You could go and live in a cabin in the woods (and that actually sounds nice), or you could still live in our modern society, but find ways to escape materialism.

Here are some suggestions:

- **Limit television**. Do you really enjoy watching TV for hours? Think about which shows you really, really love, and only watch during that time. When the commercials come on, go do something else. Or use Tivo to watch TV. You can even give up cable TV entirely, if you're brave — I have, and it's one of the best things I've ever done.

- **Eschew the news**. Journalists will never tell you this, but if they're completely honest, they'll confess that the most important part of any news company, from TV or radio news to Internet or print new, is the advertising division. It's the division that pays the paychecks of the rest of the company. The news is important in driving traffic to the advertising. So when you're watching or reading news, you're really being sucked in to advertising. Try this instead: boycott the news for a week. I've done it for about two years, and it hasn't hurt me a bit. In fact, it's helped me a lot.

- **Limit Internet reading**. I'm not saying you should cancel your cable Internet subscription or anything. I love reading blogs. But find just those that you truly love reading, that give you the most value, and limit your reading to those. And just do it once a day, for 30 minutes or so. If you can do that, you've gone a long way towards tearing yourself away from advertising.

- **Give up magazines for books**. Magazines are also designed with advertising in mind. And they rarely give you much value. Try reading an ad-free book instead. It's a much better use of your time.

- **Don't go to the mall or Walmart**. The only purpose of these places is for you to spend money. If you just want a place to spend your Saturday afternoon, find a place where you don't need to spend money to have fun — a park or a beach, for example. If you need to buy something, go to a single store (not the mall) and go in and get what you need. Don't browse and walk around looking at stuff. You'll get sucked in.

- **Monitor your urges**. When you're online, or watching TV, or at a store, keep track of the number of times you want to buy something. Keep a little notebook or index card, and just put tally marks. Once you become more aware of your urges to buy things, you can start to control them. If you could control them, limiting your consumption of media (see above tips) isn't really necessary — although I would argue that it still gives you a better quality of life.

- **Use a 30-day list**. If you still really want to buy something, put it on a list, and write down the date you added the item to the list. Now tell yourself you cannot buy that item for 30 days. It might be difficult, but you can do it. When the 30 days have passed, if you still want it, then buy it. But you can't buy anything (besides essentials like groceries) without putting it on the list for 30 days first. Many times, our urges to buy something will pass during this waiting period.

- **Declutter**. I find it pretty amazing to see all the crap I buy over a period of years, when I go through my closets and other possessions and start getting rid of stuff I don't use or want anymore. It's a gratifying process, and at the same time, it makes me realize how useless all our consumer shopping is. I don't need any of the stuff! When you do this, you may be less likely to buy more stuff. Especially if you enjoy the decluttered look of your house as much as I do.

- **Find other forms of entertainment**. There are other things to do besides watch TV or movies or read magazines or newspapers or the Internet. Try playing sports or exercising, or playing board games or creating art or writing or reading a book. Try doing fun things with your kids or visiting relatives and other loved ones. Try volunteering with a charity. I'm sure you could come up with 100 free or cheap things to do.

- **Buy used**. When you get the urge to buy something, and you're convinced that it's needed, try finding it used instead of new. Look in thrift shops or garage sales or flea markets or similar places.

A True Path to Happiness

So, if you're able to escape materialism, how can you find true happiness? There are many ways, and each of us is different, but here are some things I suggest trying:

- **Grateful list**. Make a list of things about which you're grateful in your life. Give thanks for them daily.

- **Think positive**. Try eliminating negative thinking from your life, and thinking positive instead.

- **Small pleasures**. Make a list of small things that give you great pleasure. Sprinkle them throughout your day. Notice other small pleasures as you go through your day.

- **Kindness**. Practice random acts of kindness and compassion. Do it anonymously. Help those in need. Volunteer. Make someone smile.

- **Love**. Make an intimate connection with your loved ones. Develop your friendships. Spend time with them, converse, understand them, make them happy.

- **Health**. Exercise and eat healthy — it sounds trite, but it can bring great happiness to your   life.

- **Meaning**. It's often useful to find meaning, either through a church or spiritual way, or through those we love in life or through the things we're passionate about. Give yourself a purpose.

- **Flow**. Eliminate distractions, and really pour yourself into whatever you're doing. If it's writing an article, like this one, really put yourself into it, until you forget the outside world.

- **Know yourself**. Become attuned to what brings you happiness. Study yourself. Learn about what you love, and about your ability to love. Increase your capacity for compassion.

Chapter 20:
Practical Tips for Living the Golden Rule

"...thou shalt love thy neighbor as thyself." - Leviticus 19: - Leviticus 19:18

I love the simplicity of the Golden Rule, its tendency to make I interact with happier ... and its tendency to make me happier as well.

It's true: the rule of treating others as you would want to be treated in their place will ultimately lead to your own happiness.

Let's say that you apply the Golden Rule in all of your interactions with other people, and you help your neighbors, you treat your family with kindness, you go the extra mile for your coworkers, you help a stranger in need.

Now, those actions will undoubtedly be good for the people you help and are kind to ... but you'll also notice a strange thing. People will treat you better too, certainly. Beyond that, though, you will find a growing satisfaction in yourself, a belief in yourself, a knowledge that you are a good person and a trust in yourself.

Those are not small dividends. They are huge. And for that reason — not even considering that our world will be a better place if more people live by this rule — I recommend you make the Golden Rule a focus of your actions, and try to live by it to the extent that you can.

I will admit that there are strong arguments against the Golden Rule, that there are exceptions and logic arguments that the Golden Rule, taken to extremes, falls apart. I'm not concerned about that stuff. The truth is, on a day-to-day basis, living by the Golden Rule will make you a better person, will make those around you happier, and will make the community you live in a better place.

With that in mind, let's take a look at some practical tips for living the Golden Rule in your daily life:

1. **Practice empathy**. Make it a habit to try to place yourself in the shoes of another person. Any person. Loved ones, co-workers, people you meet on the street. Really try to understand, to the extent that you can, what it is like to be them, what they are going through, and why they do what they do.

2. **Practice compassion**. Once you can understand another person, and feel what they're going through, learn to want to end their suffering. And when you can, take even a small action to somehow ease their suffering in someway.

3. **How would you want to be treated?** The Golden Rule doesn't really mean that you should treat someone else exactly as you'd want them to treat you ... it means that you should try to imagine how they want to be treated, and do that. So when you put yourself in their shoes, ask yourself how you think they want to be treated. Ask yourself how you would want to be treated if you were in their situation. John F. Kennedy did that during the controversial days of de-segregation in the 1960s, asking white Americans to imagine being looked down upon and treated badly

based only on the color of their skin. He asked them to imagine how they would want to be treated if they were in that situation, and act accordingly towards the blacks.

4. **Be friendly**. When in doubt, follow this tip. It's usually safe to be friendly towards others. Of course, there are times when others just don't want someone acting friendly towards them, and you should be sensitive to that. You should also be friendly within the bounds of appropriateness. But who doesn't like to feel welcome and wanted?

5. **Be helpful**. This is probably one of the weaknesses of our society. Sure, there are many people who go out of their way to be helpful, and I applaud them. But in general there is a tendency to keep to yourself, and to ignore the problems of others. Don't be blind to the needs and troubles of others. Look to help even before you're asked.

6. **Be courteous in traffic**. Another weakness of our society. There are few times when we are as selfish as when we're driving. We don't want to give up the right of way, we cut people off, we honk and curse. Perhaps it's the isolation of the automobile. We certainly don't act that rude in person, most of the time. So try to be courteous in traffic.

7. **Listen to others**. Another weakness: we all want to talk, but very few of us want to listen. And yet, we all want to be listened to. So take the time to actually listen to another person, rather than just wait your turn to talk. It'll also go a long way to helping you understand others.

8. **Overcome prejudice**. We all have our prejudices, whether it's based on skin color, attractiveness, height, age, gender ... it's human nature, I guess. But try to see each person as an individual human being, with different backgrounds and needs and dreams. And try to see the commonalities between you and that person, despite your differences.

9. **Stop criticism**. We all have a tendency to criticize others, whether it's people we know or people we see on television. However, ask yourself if you would like to be criticized in that person's situation. The answer is almost always "no". So hold back your criticism, and instead learn to interact with others in a positive way.

10. **Don't control others**. It's also rare that people want to be controlled. Trust me. So don't do it. This is a difficult thing, especially if we are conditioned to control people. But when you get the urge to control, put yourself in that person's shoes. You would want freedom and autonomy and trust, wouldn't you? Give that to others then.

11. **Be a child**. The urge to control and criticize is especially strong when we are adults dealing with children. In some cases, it's necessary, of course: you don't want the child to hurt himself, for example. But in most cases, it's not. Put yourself in the shoes of that child. Remember what it was like to be a child, and to be criticized and controlled. You probably didn't like it. How would you want to be treated if you were that child?

12. **Send yourself a reminder**. Email yourself a daily reminder (use Google Calendar or memotome.com, for example) to live your life by the Golden Rule, so you don't forget.

13. **Tie a string to your finger**. Or give yourself some other reminder throughout the day so that you don't forget to follow the Golden Rule in all interactions with others. Perhaps a fake golden ring on your key chain? A tattoo? :)

14. **Post it on your wall or make it your home page**. The Golden Rule makes a great mantra, and a great poster.

15. **Rise above retaliation**. We have a tendency to strike back when we're treated badly. This is natural. Resist that urge. The Golden Rule isn't about retaliation. It's about treating others well, despite how they treat you. Does that mean you should be a doormat? No ... you have to assert your rights, of course, but you can do so in a way where you still treat others well and don't strike back just because they treated you badly first. Remember Jesus' wise (but difficult to follow) advice: turn the other cheek.

16. **Be the change**. Gandhi famously told us to be the change we want to see in the world. Well, we often think of that quote as applying to grand changes, such as poverty and racism and violence. Well, sure, it does apply to those things ... but it also applies on a much smaller scale: to all the small interactions between people. Do you want people to treat each other with more compassion and kindness? Then let it start with you. Even if the world doesn't change, at least you

have.

17. **Notice how it makes you feel**. Notice how your actions affect others, especially when you start to treat them with kindness, compassion, respect, trust, love. But also notice the change in yourself. Do you feel better about yourself? Happier? More secure? More willing to trust others, now that you trust yourself? These changes come slowly and in small increments, but if you pay attention, you'll see them.

18. **Say a prayer**. There is a prayer on the Golden Rule, attributed to Eusebius of Caesarea, that would be worth saying once a day. It includes the following lines, among others:

May I gain no victory that harms me or my opponent.

May I reconcile friends who are mad at each other.

May I, insofar as I can, give all necessary help to my friends and to all who are in need.

May I never fail a friend in trouble.

Chapter 21:
Accept Criticism with Grace and Appreciation

Every day, I get emails and comments that are amazingly positive and encouraging, and in truth these messages are the very thing that sustains my blogging. However, I also get negative comments now and then: criticism of my writing, and not nice criticism either.

How do you deal with criticism? I think the first reaction for most of us is to defend ourselves, or worse yet to lash back.

And yet, while criticism can be taken as hurtful and demoralizing, it can also be viewed in a positive way: it is honesty, and it can spur us to do better. It's an opportunity to improve.

Recently, I ran an "Ask the Readers" post asking for suggestions for improvement, after receiving a few critical emails and comments. I responded to one of the critics with a "thank you" and asked him to comment in the Ask the Readers thread.

The reader emailed me back, and here was his response:

"After sending my email, I felt I might have been a little harsh. But now, after reading your response, I think you would have the perfect qualities to write an article or two about taking criticism with grace and appreciation."

I really liked that thought, so here is that post he suggested: How to take criticism with grace and appreciation.

Stop Your First Reaction

If your first reaction is to lash back at the person giving the criticism, or to become defensive, take a minute before reacting at all. Take a deep breath, and give it a little thought.

Personally, I tend to get a little angry when I'm criticized. But I have also taught myself not to react right away. For example, I'll let a critical email sit in my inbox for at least an hour before replying. Or I'll walk away from someone instead of saying something I'll regret later.

That cooling off time allows me to give it a little more thought beyond my initial reaction. It allows logic to step in, past the emotion. I don't have anything against emotion, but when it's a negative emotion, sometimes it can cause more harm than good. So I let my emotions run their course, and then respond when I'm calmer.

Turn a Negative Into a Positive

One of the keys to my success in anything I do is my ability to find positive things in things that most people see as a negative. Sickness forces me to stop my exercise program? That's a welcome rest. Tired of my job? That's a time to rediscover what's important and to look for a better job.

Supertyphoon ruined all my possessions? This allowed me to realize that my stuff wasn't important, and to be thankful that my loved ones were still alive and safe.

You can do the same thing with criticism: find the positive in it. Sure, it may be rude and mean, but in most criticism, you can find a nugget of gold: honest feedback and a suggestion for improvement.

For example, this criticism: "You write about the same things over and over and your posts are boring and stale."

Can be read: "I need to increase the variety of my posts and find new ways of looking at old things."

That's just one example of course — you can do that with just about any criticism. Sometimes it's just someone having a bad day, but many times there's at least a grain of truth in the criticism.

See it as an opportunity to improve — and without that constant improvement, we are just sitting still. Improvement is a good thing.

Thank the Critic

Even if someone is harsh and rude, thank them. They might have been having a bad day, or maybe they're just a negative person in general. But even so, your attitude of gratitude will probably catch them off-guard.

And you know what? My habit of thanking my critics has actually won a few of them over. They became friends of mine, and eventually a couple of them became some of my biggest proponents.

All because of a simple act of saying thank you for the criticism. It's unexpected, and often appreciated.

And even if the critic doesn't take your "thank you" in a good way, it's still good to do — for yourself. It's a way of reminding yourself that the criticism was a good thing for you, a way of keeping yourself humble.

Learn from the Criticism

After seeing criticism in a positive light, and thanking the critic, don't just move on and go back to business as usual.

Actually try to improve.

That's a difficult concept for some people, because they often think that they're right no matter what. But no one is always right. You, in fact, may be wrong, and the critic may be right. So see if there's something you can change to make yourself better.

And then make that change. Actually strive to do better.

When I received criticism that my posts weren't as good as they could be, I strove to improve. I tried hard to write better posts. Now, did I actually accomplish that? That's a matter of opinion — some will say no, while others seemed to enjoy the posts. Personally, I've been rather proud of some of these posts, and I'm glad I made the extra effort.

Be the Better Person

Too many times we take criticism as a personal attack, as an insult to who we are. But it's not. Well, perhaps sometimes it is, but we don't have to take it that way. Take it as a criticism of your actions, not your person. If you do that, you can detach yourself from the criticism emotionally and see what should be done.

But the way that many of us handle the criticisms that we see as personal attacks is by attacking back. "I'm not going to let someone talk to me that way." Especially if this criticism is made in public, such as in the comments of a blog. You have to defend yourself, and attack the attacker ... right?

Wrong. By attacking the attacker, you are stooping to his level. Even if the person was mean or rude, you don't have to be the same way. You don't have to commit the same sins.

If you can rise above the petty insults and attacks, and respond in a calm and positive manner to the meat of the criticism, you will be the better person. And guess what? There are two amazing benefits of this:

1. **Others will admire you and think better of you for rising above the attack**. Especially if you remain positive and actually take the criticism well. This has happened to me, when people actually complimented me on how I handled attacking comments.

2. **You will feel better about yourself**. By participating in personal attacks, we dirty ourselves. But if we can stay above that level, we feel good about who we are. And that's the most important benefit of all.

How do you stay above the attacks and be the better person? By removing yourself from the criticism, and looking only at the actions criticized. By seeing the positive in the criticism, and trying to improve. By thanking the critic. And by responding with a positive attitude.

A quick example: Someone criticizes one of my posts by saying, "You're an idiot. I don't understand what x has to do with y."

My typical response will be to first, ignore the first sentence. And second, to say something like, "Thanks for giving me an opportunity to clarify that. I don't think I made it as clear as I should have. What x has to do with y is ... blah blah. Thanks for the great question!"

And by ignoring the insult, taking it as an opportunity to clarify, thanking the critic, using the opportunity to explain my point further, and staying positive, I have accepted the criticism with grace and appreciation. And in doing so, remained the better person, and felt great about myself.

Chapter 22:
Have Faith in Humanity, and Restore Kindness

The other day I was at the DMV here on Guam, renewing my registration for both my vehicles. I got there early, as I hate lines, but realized that I forgot an important document.

Well, the woman at the DMV saved me about an hour's worth of driving and waiting in line by paying me a kindness... she accepted my registration by interpreting the regulations in a favorable way.

And that kindness just made my day.

It's amazing what a little kindness can do for you. I drove away from the DMV with a great feeling, with a love for humanity, with a desire to do good for others and pay her kindness forward.

I've since paid my debt of gratitude forward in a bunch of ways, but it's gotten me thinking about kindness and humanity in a broader sense. I have an enormous faith in humanity ... but I think we all need to work to bring kindness back to our modern society.

While running with my sister at the local track yesterday, we were talking about kindness and courtesy in our society. My sister, Katrina, has noticed that people are less courteous and more rude to each other nowadays. They don't say simple things like "Thank you" or open doors for each other or even smile at strangers.

I'm not sure if things on this front have gotten worse in recent years, but if it has, I suspect the change isn't in people, it's in the loss of a sense of community. It's that we don't come together enough, and are separated from each other in many ways.

The Effect of Anonymity

What happens when people get in cars and then converge on the roads? For some reason, they become rude, inconsiderate jerks (for the most part). But if these same people were to meet face-to-face, and have to spend time together and get to know each other, they would most likely make an attempt at being nice, at the very least.

When we're in cars, we can barely see the other drivers. We certainly don't care what they think, and we know they don't know who we are. Sure, some people are considerate drivers, but for the most part, people are aggressive and uncaring when they're in their cars.

That's the effect of anonymity.

When we actually get to know people, we usually act differently. We want to be seen as good in other people's eyes (the social component of the human animal), and as such, we'll usually go out of our way to be nice — if we interact with the person on a personal level, not an anonymous level.

Our Divided Society

As my sister Katrina pointed out, our society is changing in a number of ways ... all of them in some way dividing us as individuals:

1. **Less religious**. A much smaller proportion of our population is religious these days, which means fewer people are going to church. This means they don't get together in the same way they used to, praying, doing community projects, getting to know each other. Some people may think that's a good thing, as they are against organized religion, but the truth is that there hasn't been a strong unifying non-secular organization emerge to take the place that church used to take in our community and in our lives.

2. **Television and other media**. Much more of our time is spent indoors these days, watching TV, playing video games, playing or working on the Internet, watching movies, etc. This means we are separated from each other. We don't get together as a community anymore, we don't play outside as much (or if we do, it's in individual ways for the most part), we don't meet face-to-face.

3. **Car society**. In the days of yore, people used to walk on the streets. People would see each other on the streets and say hi, stop and chat. Kids used to play in the streets. But cars have overrun our streets, and they are no longer safe for kids or pedestrians or bikes. We are forced into cars, because there's no better way to get around (for the most part — in some cities, mass transit is a viable alternative, but not where I live). And when we're in cars, as I mentioned above, we are

separated from our fellow human beings.

Amish Barn Raising

When I think about ways we can come together as a community, to interact in more personal and positive ways, I think of the Amish barn raising tradition. The community comes together to help a family ... this is the kind of tradition where people help each other out, get to know each other, and bond.

I think about that, and I wonder if there are ways we could get the community together, helping each other out. There are already some of these kinds of activities, such as community cleanups, Habitat for Humanity, other charity organizations, and the like. These are amazing ways to bring people together, in a common cause of helping others.

I'd like to see more of these kinds of things. I don't have the answers, but I do know that if we make an effort to organize ways to help each other out, and come together, our communities will be better off. People will get to know each other, and will be kinder to each other. That's my hope, at least.

My Faith in Humanity

Call me naive or hopelessly optimistic, but I have a very positive view of humanity. Sure, we see greed and rudeness and abuse and selfishness every day. But I believe that's more a symptom of the systems in our society, rather than of an evil human race.

I have faith in humanity.

I often leave my car doors unlocked. I carry cash around, just ready for a mugger to take it from me. I give money to people who say they need it, if I have it, not worrying about whether they'll spend it on food or drugs or whatever.

Recently a reader asked for a way to buy the Zen To Done ebook in some other way than PayPal. I didn't have a good way to do that, so I emailed him the book and asked him to mail me a check — having faith that he'd do it. Not only did he mail me a check, but he added an extra $40 to the total, with a note that the extra money was for copies he planned to give to friends and for my hard work here at Zen Habits.

That guy made my day. He proved that my faith in humanity is justified. I keep his note in the book I'm reading as a bookmark, so that I see it several times a day.

You guys, the readers of Zen Habits, are incredibly giving, kind, encouraging, supportive, generous.

I meet people every day who are friendly, who do me kindnesses, who lift my spirits.

Humanity is a wonderful thing. People are amazing, beautiful creatures.

What we need are ways to bring out the best in people. To bring them together. To have them help each other, instead of trying to outdo each other.

We need freer systems, instead of the authoritarian ones that oppress us now. We need cooperative systems, instead of the competitive ones we have now. We need unifying systems, instead of the divisive ones that exist today.

We need change. And as Gandhi famously said,

"We must be the change we want to see in the world."

I hope to be that change. I hope you will too.

Chapter 23:
Boost Your Self-Confidence

"Once we believe in ourselves, we can risk curiosity, wonder, spontaneous delight, or any experience that reveals the human spirit." - E.E. Cummings

One of the things that held me back from pursuing my dreams for many years was fear of failure ... and the lack of self-confidence that I needed to overcome that fear.

It's something we all face, to some degree, I think. The key question: how do you overcome that fear?

By working on your self-confidence and self-esteem. Without really thinking of it in those terms, that's what I've been doing over the years, and that's what helped me finally overcome my fears, and finally pursue my dreams.

I still have those fears, undoubtedly. But now I know that I can beat them, that I can break through that wall of fear and come out on the other side. I've done it many times now, and that success will fuel further success.

This post was inspired by reader Nick from Finland, who asked for an article about self-worth and self-confidence: "Many of the things you propose make people feel better about themselves and actually help building self-confidence. However, I would be interested on reading your input in general on this topic. Taking time out for your own plans and dreams, doing things another way than most other people and generally not necessarily

'fitting in' can be quite hard with a low self-confidence."
Truer words have never been spoken. It's near impossible
to make time for your dreams, to break free from the
traditional mold, and to truly be yourself, if you have low
self-esteem and self-confidence.

As an aside, I know that some people make a strong
distinction between self-esteem and self-confidence. In
this article, I use them interchangeably, even if there is a
subtle but perhaps important difference ... the difference
being whether you believe you're worthy of respect from
others (self-esteem) and whether you believe in yourself
(self-confidence). In the end, both amount to the same
thing, and in the end, the actions I mention below give a
boost to both self-esteem and self-confidence.

Taking control of your self-confidence

If you are low in self-confidence, is it possible to do
things that will change that? Is your self-
confidence in your control? While it may not seem so, if
you are low in self-confidence, I strongly believe that you
can do things to increase your self-confidence. It is not
genetic, and you do not have to be reliant on
others to increase your self-confidence. And if you believe
that you are not very competent, not very smart, not very
attractive, etc. ... that can be changed.

You can become someone worthy of respect, and someone
who can pursue what he wants despite the naysaying of
others.

You can do this by taking control of your life, and taking
control of your self-confidence. By taking concrete
actions that improve your competence, your self-image,

you can increase that self-confidence, without the help of anyone else.

Below, I outline 25 things that will help you do that. None of them is revolutionary, none of them will do it all by themselves. The list certainly isn't comprehensive. These are just some of my favorite things, stuff that's worked for me.

And you don't need to do all of them, as if this were a recipe ... pick and choose those that appeal to you, maybe just a couple at first, and give them a try. If they work, try others. If they don't, try others.

Here they are, in no particular order:

1. **Groom yourself**. This seems like such an obvious one, but it's amazing how much of a difference a shower and a shave can make in your feelings of self-confidence and for your self-image. There have been days when I turned my mood around completely with this one little thing.

2. **Dress nicely**. A corollary of the first item above ... if you dress nicely, you'll feel good about yourself. You'll feel successful and presentable and ready to tackle the world. Now, dressing nicely means something different for everyone ... it doesn't necessarily mean wearing a $500 outfit, but could mean casual clothes that are nice looking and presentable.

3. **Photoshop your self-image**. Our self-image means so much to us, more than we often realize. We have a mental picture of ourselves, and it determines how

confident we are in ourselves. But this picture isn't fixed and immutable. You can change it. Use your mental Photoshopping skills, and work on your self-image. If it's not a very good one, change it. Figure out why you see yourself that way, and find a way to fix it.

4. **Think positive**. One of the things I learned when I started running, about two years ago, what how to replace negative thoughts (see next item) with positive ones. How I can actually change my thoughts, and by doing so make great things happened. With this tiny little skill, I was able to train for and run a marathon within a year. It sounds so trite, so Norman Vincent Peale, but my goodness this works. Seriously. Try it if you haven't.

5. **Kill negative thoughts**. Goes hand-in-hand with the above item, but it's so important that I made it a separate item. You have to learn to be aware of your self-talk, the thoughts you have about yourself and what you're doing. When I was running, sometimes my mind would start to say, "This is too hard. I want to stop and go watch TV." Well, I soon learned to recognize this negative self-talk, and soon I learned a trick that changed everything in my life: I would imagine that a negative thought was a bug, and I would vigilantly be on the lookout for these bugs. When I caught one, I would stomp on it (mentally of course) and squash it. Kill it dead. Then replace it with a positive one. ("C'mon, I can do this! Only one mile left!")

"Know yourself and you will win all battles."
- Sun Tzu

6. **Get to know yourself**. When going into battle, the wisest general learns to know his enemy very, very well. You can't defeat the enemy without knowing him. And when you're trying to overcome a negative self-image and replace it with self-confidence, your enemy is yourself. Get to know yourself well. Start listening to your thoughts. Start writing a journal about yourself, and about the thoughts you have about yourself, and analyzing why you have such negative thoughts. And then think about the good things about yourself, the things you can do well, the things you like. Start thinking about your limitations, and whether they're real limitations or just ones you've allowed to be placed there, artificially. Dig deep within yourself, and you'll come out (eventually) with even greater self-confidence.

7. **Act positive**. More than just thinking positive, you have to put it into action. Action, actually, is the key to developing self-confidence. It's one thing to learn to think positive, but when you start acting on it, you change yourself, one action at a time. You are what you do, and so if you change what you do, you change what you are. Act in a positive way, take action instead of telling yourself you can't, be positive. Talk to people in a positive way, put energy into your actions. You'll soon start to notice a difference.

8. **Be kind and generous**. Oh, so corny. If this is too corny for you, move on. But for the rest of you, know that being kind to others, and generous with yourself and your time and what you have, is a tremendous way to improve your self-image. You act in accordance with the Golden Rule, and you start to feel

127

good about yourself, and to think that you are a good person. It does wonders for your self-confidence, believe me.

"One important key to success is self-confidence. A key to self-confidence is preparation." - Arthur Ashe

9. **Get prepared.** It's hard to be confident in yourself if you don't think you'll do well at something. Beat that feeling by preparing yourself as much as possible. Think about taking an exam: if you haven't studied, you won't have much confidence in your abilities to do well on the exam. But if you studied your butt off, you're prepared, and you'll be much more confident. Now think of life as your exam, and prepare yourself.

10. **Know your principles and live them**. What are the principles upon which your life is built? If you don't know, you will have trouble, because your life will feel directionless. For myself, I try to live the Golden Rule (and fail often). This is my key principle, and I try to live my life in accordance with it. I have others, but they are mostly in some way related to this rule (the major exception being to "Live my Passion"). Think about your principles ... you might have them but perhaps you haven't given them much thought. Now think about whether you actually live these principles, or if you just believe in them but don't act on them.

11. **Speak slowly**. Such a simple thing, but it can have a big difference in how others perceive you. A person in authority, with authority, speaks slowly. It shows confidence. A person who feels that he isn't worth listening to will speak quickly, because he doesn't

want to keep others waiting on something not worthy of listening to. Even if you don't feel the confidence of someone who speaks slowly, try doing it a few times. It will make you feel more confident. Of course, don't take it to an extreme, but just don't sound rushed either.

12. **Stand tall**. I have horrible posture, so it will sound hypocritical for me to give this advice, but I know it works because I try it often. When I remind myself to stand tall and straight, I feel better about myself. I imagine that a rope is pulling the top of my head toward the sky, and the rest of my body straightens accordingly. As an aside, people who stand tall and confident are more attractive. That's a good thing any day, in my book.

13. **Increase competence**. How do you feel more competent? By becoming more competent. And how do you do that? By studying and practicing. Just do small bits at a time. If you want to be a more competent writer, for example, don't try to tackle the entire profession of writing all at once. Just begin to write more. Journal, blog, write short stories, do some freelance writing. The more you write, the better you'll be. Set aside 30 minutes a day to write (for example), and the practice will increase your competence.

14. **Set a small goal and achieve it**. People often make the mistake of shooting for the moon, and then when they fail, they get discouraged. Instead, shoot for something much more achievable. Set a goal you know you can achieve, and then achieve it. You'll feel good about that. Now set another small goal and

achieve that. The more you achieve small goals, the better you'll be at it, and the better you'll feel. Soon you'll be setting bigger (but still achievable) goals and achieving those too.

15. **Change a small habit**. Not a big one, like quitting smoking. Just a small one, like writing things down. Or waking up 10 minutes earlier. Or drinking a glass of water when you wake up. Something small that you know you can do. Do it for a month. When you've accomplished it, you'll feel like a million bucks.

16. **Focus on solutions**. If you are a complainer, or focus on problems, change your focus now. Focusing on solutions instead of problems is one of the best things you can do for your confidence and your career. "I'm fat and lazy!" So how can you solve that? "But I can't motivate myself!" So how can you solve that? "But I have no energy!" So what's the solution?

17. **Smile**. Another trite one. But it works. I feel instantly better when I smile, and it helps me to be kinder to others as well. A little tiny thing that can have a chain reaction. Not a bad investment of your time and energy.

18. **Volunteer**. Related to the "be kind and generous" item above, but more specific. It's the holiday season right now ... can you find the time to volunteer for a good cause, to spread some holiday cheer, to make the lives of others better? It'll be some of the best time you've ever spent, and an amazing side benefit is that you'll feel better about yourself, instantly.

19. **Be grateful**. I'm a firm believer in gratitude, as

anyone who's been reading this blog for very long knows well. But I put it here because while being grateful for what you have in life, for what others have given you, is a very humbling activity ... it can also be a very positive and rewarding activity that will improve your self-image.

20. **Exercise**. Gosh, I seem to put this one on almost every list. But if I left it off this list I would be doing you a disservice. Exercise has been one of my most empowering activities in the last couple years, and it has made me feel so much better about myself. All you have to do is take a walk a few times a week, and you'll see benefits. Start the habit.

21. **Empower yourself with knowledge**. Empowering yourself, in general, is one of the best strategies for building self-confidence. You can do that in many ways, but one of the surest ways to empower yourself is through knowledge. This is along the same vein as building competence and getting prepared ... by becoming more knowledgeable, you'll be more confident ... and you become more knowledgeable by doing research and studying. The Internet is a great tool, of course, but so are the people around you, people who have done what you want, books, magazines, and educational institutions.

22. **Do something you've been procrastinating on**. What's on your to-do list that's been sitting there? Do it first thing in the morning, and get it out of the way. You'll feel great about yourself.

23. **Get active**. Doing something is almost always better than not doing anything. Of course, doing something

could lead to mistakes ... but mistakes are a part of life. It's how we learn. Without mistakes, we'd never get better. So don't worry about those. Just do something. Get off your butt and get active — physically, or active by taking steps to accomplish something.

24. **Work on small things**. Trying to take on a huge project or task can be overwhelming and daunting and intimidating for anyone, even the best of us. Instead, learn to break off small chunks and work in bursts. Small little achievements make you feel good, and they add up to big achievements. Learn to work like this all the time, and soon you'll be a self-confident maniac.

25. **Clear your desk**. This might seem like a small, simple thing (then again, for some of you it might not be so small). But it has always worked wonders for me. If my desk starts to get messy, and the world around me is in chaos, clearing off my desk is my way of getting a little piece of my life under control. It is the calm in the center of the storm around me.

"Somehow I can't believe that there are any heights that can't be scaled by a man who knows the secrets of making dreams come true. This special secret, it seems to me, can be summarized in four Cs. They are curiosity, confidence, courage, and constancy, and the greatest of all is confidence. When you believe in a thing, believe in it all the way, implicitly and unquestionable."

- Walt Disney

Chapter 24:
Live Your Life Consciously

"A life lived of choice is a life of conscious action. A life lived of chance is a life of unconscious creation."
- Neale Donald Walsch

As much as possible, I try to live my life by bringing to my consciousness what is bubbling up from my unconsciousness.

I try to clear the fog through which we often drift, to see where I'm going, to make conscious choices instead of automatic ones.

Do you ever have a feeling that you're drifting through life, and not going where you want to go? Or that you don't know how you got where you are today?

Living consciously is about taking control of your life, about thinking about your decisions rather than making them without thought, about having a life that we want rather than settling for the one that befalls us.

If you're drifting through life, or feel out of control, or don't know how you got here ... deciding to live consciously could be the single most important thing you do.

Are you living unconsciously now?

Ask yourself the following questions ... if you find yourself saying yes to many of them, you might want to consider trying conscious living:

1. **Are you in a job that you fell into rather than the job you want?**

2. **Are you doing things that are given to you rather than what you love to do?**

3. **Are you spending your time doing busy work rather than what you want to do with your days?**

4. **Do you wish you could spend more time with loved ones?**

5. **Do you find yourself overweight because you've been eating the food you've been eating for years and stuck in a rut of not exercising?**

6. **Do you find yourself living from paycheck to paycheck or in debt, not knowing where your money goes?**

7. **Do you find yourself wasting your time doing things that aren't important rather than focusing on completing the things that are very important?**

8. **Do you go through your days not thinking about what you want out of life and how to get it?**

If you answered "no" to all of these questions, you're probably already living consciously, and you don't need this article at all. For those who would like to live more consciously, read on.

How to Live Life Consciously

It's not something you can change overnight. Living consciously is a lifestyle, a skill, an art. It's not something you do just once, but a habit that you can form for the rest of your life.

But it is deceptively simple: Be conscious, and think about everything you do. Make conscious choices rather than doing things without thinking. That's all.

It sounds simple, but it's amazing how few people actually do this, and it's amazing how easy it is to live life on autopilot, and just do what we always do because that's what we're used to doing. And it's easier that way, even if our lives are difficult.

It's not easy to changes our lives, to break out of our routines, to begin to live the lives we want. It takes willful effort, energy and constant vigilance to think about our choices ... all of them.

Here are some key tips that have worked for me:

1. **Make reflecting on your life a regular routine**. Whether you keep a journal, or make reflecting on your day part of your evening routine, or have a weekly session where you review your life or take some time away from the office to reflect on everything ... it's important that you give things some thought. Regularly.

2. **At least once a year, set or review your life's goals**.

What do you want to do in life? What is important to you? What do you want your life to be like? And how will you get there? Write it down, and keep it somewhere you will see it often, and take action.

3. **Also review your relationships**. The people we love are among the most important things in our lives, if not the only important things. You need to think about your relationships. Do you spend enough time with them? Do you show your appreciation for them? Is there a way you can improve your relationship? Do you need to forgive or apologize about anything? Are there barriers that can be removed? Communication that can be improved? Also review your relationships with others, such as co-workers.

4. **Consider your impact on the world**. How does what you do, what you consume, and how you live, impact the environment? How does it impact poor people in Third World countries? How does it impact the poor, the powerless, the voiceless? How does it impact your community? Your life has an impact, whether you think about it or not. Being conscious of how your decisions affect others is important.

5. **Consider the real costs of each purchase**. We often buy things without really thinking about what we're doing or what they really cost. Sure, it's just $30 ... no problem, right? But that $30 might represent several hours of your life ... hours that you'll never get back. Do you really want to spend your life earning money for trivial purchases? Is that what you want to do with your life? Worth some thought, I think.

6. **Consider the real costs of the things in your life**. Our lives are filled with stuff ... our houses, our offices ... and beyond just the cost of buying the stuff, this stuff takes a toll on us. The stuff in our life must be arranged, cleaned, moved, taken with us when we move ... it takes up the space in our life, it is visual stress. Later, we'll have to get rid of it, sort through all of it, take time to throw it away or recycle it or donate it. If having the stuff is not worth all of that, then get rid of it.

7. **Review how you spend your time**. Until we do a time audit, and keep a log of our day, even if it's just for one or two days, we don't really know how we spend our time. And if we do audit our time, it can be very surprising. And if we know how we're spending our time now, we can make conscious decisions to change how we spend our time in the future.

8. **Explore yourself**. Not in a dirty way. Take some time to think about what kind of person you are. What your values are. Whether you live your life according to those values. How you treat people. How you treat yourself. Think about this: what do you want people to say about you when you die?

Acknowledgments

For their patient support of all my work, I would like to thank my wife, Eva, and my kids: Chloe, Justin, Rain, Maia, Seth and Noelle.

For their encouragement, thanks are also owed to my sister Katrina and my mom, Shannon, to whom this book is dedicated. Love to all my other families.

This book is also dedicated to the readers of Zen Habits, who have made all my dreams come true.

Charlie Pabst of CharfishDesign.com, the excellent designer of the digital version of this book, deserves heaps of praise for his work.

8880602R0

Made in the USA
Lexington, KY
09 March 2011